A Thousand Laurie Lees

The Centenary Celebration of a Man and a Valley

Adam Horovitz
with illustrations by Jo Sanders and
photographs by Dan Brown

The
History
Press

To the memory of Frances Horovitz, 1938–83, and Laurie Lee, 1914–97

Monoprint illustrations © Jo Sanders
Photographs © Dan Brown

First published 2014

The History Press
The Mill, Brimscombe Port
Stroud, Gloucestershire, GL5 2QG
www.thehistorypress.co.uk

British Library Cataloguing in Publication Data.
A catalogue record for this book is available from the British Library.

ISBN 978 0 7509 5376 4

Typesetting and origination by The History Press
Printed in Great Britain

Contents

Acknowledgements

My thanks to The Society of Authors for the support provided by a Society of Authors' Authors' Foundation grant (www.societyofau-thors.org).

The writing of this book would not have been possible without the generosity of Jacqueline Kroft, who let me stay at her house to write the first section of the book, and of the Painswick Quakers for giving me access to their exquisite Meeting House, where I was able to write several more chapters. I am also grateful to the Greenshop in Bisley and to my editor, Shaun Barrington, for their patience and understanding. Thanks also to Karen Walker for her careful, considered and helpful readings of the manuscript and to my father, Michael Horovitz, for his contributions to the fluidity of text and memory. Thanks also to Jane Percival for the use of her painting and to Patricia Hopf, whose book *The Turbulent History of a Cotswold Valley* (Nonsuch, 2006) was an invaluable resource during the writing of this book. Thanks are also due to Andrew Wood for showing me the photograph of Diana Lodge, and to Jessie Ann Matthew for allowing me to use it at such short notice.

I would particularly like to thank Jo Sanders for her illustrations and Dan Brown for his photographs, which have made this book such a joy to look at, as well as Mark Anderson, who provided the title of this book many years ago.

Thanks are also due to Joe and Imogen Reeve, Anne Garcin and Nik Bragg, Rick Vick, Alex Jamieson, Brian and Carole Oosthuysen, Francoise Pinteaux-Jones, Isa Clee-Cadman and Gavin McClafferty and Anne and Ian Mackintosh, who looked after me when I broke my arms ten days after signing the contract to write this book and whose generosity allowed me the space and time to rethink it as I mended.

'An Owl Breaks the Silence' was originally published in John Papworth's *Fourth World Review* (1989) and then in *Grandchildren of Albion* (New Departures, 1992). 'Earth Song' first appeared in *Earth Ascending* (Stride, 1996). 'Burials' and 'At This Time' first appeared in *Oral* (Sceptre, 1999). A version of 'Roots' first appeared in issue 1 of *Bare Fiction* magazine (2013).

'Burials' and 'Cheese Kisses' are published in Adam Horovitz's collection *Turning* (2011), and reprinted with the permission of Headland Publications.

Extracts from Frances Horovitz's poetry appear courtesy of Bloodaxe Books, taken from Frances Horovitz, *Collected Poems: New Edition* (Bloodaxe Books, 2011).

Quotes from Laurie Lee's poetry are taken from his *Selected Poems* (Andre Deutsch Ltd, 1983) and are reproduced with the permission of his estate.

The quote attributed to John Papworth is taken from *Frances Horovitz, Poet: A Symposium*, edited by Father Brocard Sewell (Aylesford Press, 1987).

The quote attributed to Laurie Lee regarding the development of the Slad Valley is taken from *Laurie Lee: The Well-Loved Stranger* by Valerie Grove (Viking Penguin, 1999).

The extract from *Midsummer Morning Jog Log* by Michael Horovitz is used courtesy of Five Seasons Press.

Introduction

The Night of a Thousand Laurie Lees

Into the quiet of the valley the drunken cyclists came roaring, dressed all in white, veering across the road like baffled owls, tearing up the stillness of the May twilight, disturbing bats in their feeding dance and drowning out the last low hum of fleeing insects. Singing and shouting they came, all dressed as Laurie Lee, fedoras jammed on their heads, tilting at the Woolpack pub as if it were a squat stone windmill. In their pockets were books, any books they could lay their hands on. *The Observer Book of Dogs*, something by Barbara Cartland. It didn't matter so long as it was a book.

The pub was humming gently along as it always did in the early evening on the outskirts of the tourist season; a few locals propped at the bar chewing their way through Uley ale or Old Rosie cider which, if it wasn't drunk quickly enough, tended to simmer in the barrel until it became a sort of explosive West Country Calvados that tore at taste buds and brain cells and, later on, the sides of cars taken home by incautious drivers. Dave the landlord was more than likely stooped by the battered till as usual, barking with laughter at the bawdy jokes that swim gasping for reaction through any bar where everyone knows everyone else.

The Woolpack was a delightfully battered and quasi-homely place in 1998, a year after Laurie Lee died. A simple kitchen lurked behind the stairs to the apartment above, ready to catch the tourists if they were exhausted from long walks through the steep valley, or to feed the hungry natives if they were desperate to escape their own kitchens.

Downstairs, through the dark cellar where a lonely fruit machine lingered dolefully amongst bashed and aged firkins of ale, there was a pool table for the younger generation to hang out at, sucking slowly at thin roll-ups and making a couple of pints last the whole night. Sometimes, if the pub was quiet and they were very quick, enterprising couples would hang out on the table half in their clothes, keeping a weather ear open for the creak of the door, the heavy footsteps of someone coming down to change the lines.

It was a place where nothing much happened, other than the usual mythologising, the arguments about football, politics or the price of eggs or the occasional lonely old man in his cups who blew beer froth through his beard as he clumsily entreated the latest pretty young pot girl to come home with him. He usually went home happy if the expected 'No!' came with a gentle smile. No one left in the pub had ever quite achieved Laurie's sly, twinkling charm, although many tried to reincarnate it.

On The Night of a Thousand Laurie Lees, however, a little anarchy and devilment was coming back, careering down the road from Miserden, from Frank Mansell's old pub The Carpenter's Arms where the drinking had begun in earnest, carried on battered bicycles and powered by laughter and beer.

Imagine, if you will, the bikes being steered through a long line of cars parked on the road; the concerned lights blinking sleepily on in the old schoolhouse as riders curse and topple and laugh at the clumsiness of their arrival. The machines being parked huggermugger against the solid metal fence, there to prevent drunks from falling into the beer garden. The wheels tangled with pedals, feet and brambles. One bicycle narrowly avoiding the steep careen down the steps to the outside lavatory – slippery, uneven slabs that have cricked the backs of many an unwary drinker over the years.

Silence in the pub as a football chant ('Laurie LEE Laurie LEE Laurie LEE-EE!') goes up outside, building in rounds before it blows in through the door followed by a number of men dressed as Laurie and thrusting books into the faces of the bewildered drinkers. 'Signed books available!' barks one of the Lauries, scribbling in *The Observer Book of Dogs* and putting it down amidst the pints on the nearest table. 'Drinks available.'

More Lauries enter, all signing books, adjusting their hats and husking out requests for beer, their tongues parched with the effort of song and cycling. The bar fills, bodies pressed against each other in a scrum for drink. The locals are crowded into pockets of confusion, subsumed by Lauries. Laughter and song swell like a bubble, bursting from the window behind the bar that overlooks Swift's Hill, the woodland Laurie bought years ago with the profits from *Cider with Rosie*, and sinks down the hill to Laurie's house where his widow and daughter, Kathy and Jessy, are remembering Laurie with a gathering of friends, marking the first anniversary of his death.

They are drawn up the hill from their quieter memories by the chanting, the echo of Laurie's name bouncing off the bruised old stone of the cottages. Over the car park they come, stepping carefully on the erratic stairs past the lavatory and in through the Woolpack's door. The painted packhorse sign swings in the breeze, its creak obliterated. The valley feels empty. All life is gathered in the pub, anarchic and beery.

The many arms of Laurie open in welcome as Kathy enters the pub. Books are dropped and drinks passed around, charged and recharged. Laurie suddenly seems alive and well and living on in the valley's dreaming, in the mouths and minds of everyone who lives there or passes through, bound into the landscape like a white clad Jack-in-the-Green.

The Slad Valley has been bound in, farmed and fenced by literature for as long as I can remember, one of a few Southern English rural idylls to have survived semi-intact into the twenty-first century without succumbing entirely to the deathly creep of empty commuterism.

The quiet boundaries of Laurie Lee's Edwardian upbringing, through which news or the occasional deserter from distant wars crept furtive and wary, have gone. Broadband has opened wider than the sky the horizons of this small, glacier-cut valley, fringed though it still is by an endless quiff of deciduous trees.

It is a place of quiet mystery in its deepest recesses, with the contentment of a blurry feudal ease at its surface, into which the wider world bounds irregularly like a large, alarming dog only to be rebuffed – or, better still, absorbed with a game of fetch-the-stick. Landowners and workers rub shoulders in the valley's heart: the pub. Even modern celebrities, whose notoriously unwieldy egos can easily destabilise any community into which they move, are moving to the outlying villages and country houses and being subsumed by Slad.

Slad is place that exists curiously out of time, like the sort of fantastical land I read about as a child (when I wasn't chasing off into the valley after butterflies, or looking for sheep skulls and badger setts) where dimensions in time and space would interlock. The tattered remnants of rural hierarchy coexist with patchy mobile signal, sleek celebrity alongside scuff-booted workman, artist alongside merchant banker. The past intrudes on the present. Even the sort of idyllic hippy upbringing I had in a thumb offshoot of the valley to which my parents moved in 1971, out beyond the farmhouse racing stables, still exists in places, free from creeping urban paranoia, streetlights and the imperative of labour to the exclusion of dreaming.

I

The Apple's Rounded World

Behold the apples' rounded worlds:
juice-green of July rain,
the black polestar of flowers, the rind
mapped with its crimson stain.

From 'Apples' by Laurie Lee

Things are changing. A year lost to sorrow recedes into the distance and I am cleaning up and clearing out the house in which I grew up. A time of stepping back and moving on. There is a great deal of work to be done sifting and sorting papers; my father's archive needs taming and ordering, as does mine. There is such a lot of it, much-layered with dust in the further reaches of the attic. Dust and the early history of the counterculture; books and memories spider-webbed in glass.

On the one clear day of the Jubilee bank holiday, I have come with friends to the house. They are gardening. The garden needs as much ordering as the archive – it is a church of little light under the steepling trees.

I dive into the wealth of papers and begin to clear some space. The long day passes in dust clouds, which dance like long-lost faces on the edge of daylight. My father has returned to London when suddenly, in amongst a pile of addled, raddled and mouse-ridden jiffy bags, I discover a cache of handwritten manuscripts of my mother's poetry, only one of which the mice had got to: a poem of hers about a Peruvian flute carved from human bone – it too had been shaved down to the essentials – and a collection of photographs. Of us. Of the family, all my life ago.

In the photos, I too am shaved down to the essence of existence – I must be three months old. These are the photos taken when we moved to the cottage, out of London to this branching out of the valley at the heart of *Cider with Rosie* country. The house, heavy in the here and now with jasmine, boxed in by privet and yew and beech, also looks bare and young and clean.

My parents too; they hold their bodies like saplings, my mother sharp and fluid as a willow, my father a little more knotted, with a beard as tenacious as ivy. The land is bare; an apple tree, a few distant saplings; light. The black and white prints are bleached with age; only a few figures stand out in dark relief.

I am caked in dust, encased in a skin of the past, sat at the top of the narrow curve of attic stairwell, my tea going cold. In the distance I hear chainsaws and laughter, the noise of change. I get up and go downstairs. In the front room, the new curtains are drawn. I walk to the front door and find myself surrounded by light, lifted out of dusty reflection of the past and into its daylight.

One small section of the garden has travelled backwards, has been shaved down to that earlier state. Photographs and present day have merged in palimpsest. The yew trees lour above us, yet this is still a small, bare but fruitful Eden – the earth is dark and rich with neglect, the brutal, invasive stems of nettle and mint are tamed. The apple tree has been cut down. New knowledge needs planting out.

Memories are hardy as seeds; you plant them young and watch them grow in unexpected directions, germinating and cross-pollinating until a full-grown plant shadows everything you remember. Nothing ever grows into quite the shapes you expect or hope for.

As I grow older, remembering my mother in the valley in which I grew up, lost in the intense heat of the summers that book-ended gloriously cold, brief winters where snow piled up on the narrow, walled lane twice as high as myself, the memories of her creep through me like ivy through a dry-stone wall. They clutch at and change my perception, and the landscape becomes darker.

I am too young, perhaps, to remember arriving in the valley, or to see Slad over the tops of saplings and through close-cropped fields of cattle and sheep through anything other than the photographer's faded lens, but I remember the sensation of belonging that rippled through me as I waded in bright red boots through the ford in the stream, heading up to the badger sett at the edge of Catswood, or as I basked beneath the Roman bridge playing high-pitched troll to any passing gruff two-legged goat.

The valley was my mother's then, and I'd have defended it and her with all the animal instinct and animosity a three-year-old can rustle up; would have waded to the Octopus Tree downstream from Snows Farm, in whose flailing roots I nestled as if holding some sort of fort against the threat of invasion, would have baaed and mooed and waved my sticks (which dreamt of being weapons) at passing livestock or at wasps until, laughing, my mother picked me up, clutched me to her shiny black quilted walking coat and hauled me home through the young, narrow woods which grew up through jaw-line husks of dry-stone walls, as the dark came down and intermittent lights flicked on one by one in dark corners of the valley.

The valley was my playpen; bound in by walls and fences, I was safe to run and, as I grew, run further within the square mile or so of Slad Valley that was mine, that idyllic Venn confusion point where the parishes of Painswick and Bisley meet; it was never certain to the outside world where it was exactly that one lived.

When I answered the phone aged three or four, running determinedly towards the new technology, as all children do when presented with alluring adult toys, I remember speaking into the receiver, in the clear tones I had learned from my mother, that this was Painswick, followed by the four-digit number that was ours alone. Or almost ours alone, because I also remember the way that sometimes, mysteriously, other voices would appear on the party line, incomprehensibly not there to talk to me. I would listen, intrigued, and pipe up with question and complaint until my mother came to restore my peace (and theirs) and take the telephone away.

The apple tree that is now gone, seasoning slowly for the fire in this suddenly forested garden, is the first thing I truly remember of early childhood, outside my yellow bedroom speckled with stars and the intense universe of my mother's arms. It was my grotto, that apple tree, my small church hung with laundry, mirrors, fruit. It bore apples that burst still in my mouth like dreams. It fruited year round until I was five, I'm certain of that.

The photos from the attic are stuck into collages like eyes gummed up with sleep. There are photos of me, my large head curtained in a wisp of gold that Rumpelstiltskin might have spun, lurching up the slight slope beneath the apple boughs and wearing a smile whose cherubic nature is sullied slightly by a smear of mud, or the pulp of fruit – the process of peeling these pictures apart makes it hard to be sure. Photos of my mother, smiling through elderflower; of my father, laughing, gnomic, bearded as Pan; of lovers, family, friends. All of us play second fiddle to the valley in these photos, poor players in a stage of its growth, a small harmonious chorus to its relentless song.

It was music that brought us here, the alluring song of the country-side that called so many of the beatnik and hippy generation away from the cities. Certainly, the strident operatics of London were too much for my mother to bear. She had grown up in 'shabby' wartime Walthamstow and run to the edges of Epping Forest to erect altars to Pan as a teenager, urgent to escape the suburban confines of her parents' aspirations and the depredations of rationing. My father, 'incorrigibly urban' according to Robert Graves, dreamed the same dream (at least for a while) and found a cottage, advertised in the *Evening Standard* as 'going for a song'.

For two poets of the hopeful 1960s bound up in the music of lan-guage and at least one of them keening to escape the high towers of London, this was enough – a song was pretty much all they could afford. Yet it was the song that bought them and brought them; this was a valley they had visited before, had known in walks and dreams and trips of all varieties, getting out of London in the comedown years of the 1960s to befriend and stay with the artist Diana Lodge at Trillgate, calling on John Papworth, the founder of Resurgence, in Elcombe and, completing a wonky and arbitrary geographical and artistic triangle that became a rough-cut diamond when we moved in to our mullion-windowed cottage, Laurie Lee, whom my father had met in London around jazz and poetry gigs and at the Chelsea Arts Club and bohemian parties around the capital.

The valley was alive with musics: the curdling, piercing soprano scream of vixens, the angry punkish bark of jays, the wind dragging its endless fugue in green through the trees. It infiltrated everything, penetrating the stone walls of our cottage as if they were paper, leading words in a new dance. It seemed as if my parents had stepped into some sweet-scented Arcadia built out of Blake's *Songs of Innocence*.

No Arcadia is complete without people. At the end of our garden, which comprised a quarter-acre stretch partitioned into sunlight and a hill of trees and watched over by the triple-eyed mullion arches that gave the cottage its name, lived Bill, ancient to my young eyes, though he can't have been more than twenty. He was living in the old chapel in the very early days of my life and I remember him striding across the garden in heavy boots, a big friendly presence with a cat called Bilbo stalking the long grasses and nettles behind him, wary of our cat, Arwen, so called because she had a small white evening star on her pitch black chest, like the Evenstar in *The Lord of the Rings*.

When my father was away, which was often in those early days, in London or America for readings, Bill was there to help with house repairs, or to flirt, or both. I remember my mother leaping from the bath to pull down the yellow and orange floral blind when she realised that Bill was climbing the ladder to fix the flat roof; her half-angry, half-amused expression at the wolf whistles that her sudden and brief display of nakedness elicited as she slid back into the bath.

CHEESE KISSES

In a bright kitchen the colour of custard
the black cat's curling out of a yawn
on the long pine table,
spread for the beginnings of a meal.

The oven is hot and creaking.
She turns to it, dons her striped blue and grey apron.
Hair hides her face as she bends to check the baking,
all but her eyes, which laugh at me.

A knock at the door. *Come in*, she calls.
Bill swings in smiling
the muck of gardens on his boots
She turns, rests against the cooker, greets him warmly.

He still away? asks Bill. A nod, hair bobbing, and a smile.
I watch in silence as the game begins.
Too young to call it flirting,
all I know is that I've been sidelined.

I watch, jealous, tease the cat.
There is fire suddenly –
her apron strings have caught
on the hob. My mother's backside is on fire.

Bill swings her round, slaps.
The fire goes out. There is silence in the kitchen,
but for my laughter, asking for the trick
to be worked again.

Bill leaves quickly.
Out of the oven
come cheese kisses
which melt in my mouth only.

I soon realised, jealously, that my opinion was not just a child's nat-ural, bonded opinion of his mother. Other men than Bill came visit-ing when she was alone with me in the valley. Some came hopeful, bearing gifts. Ossie, the photographer who brought the black cat down from London when I was one year old, adored her and named the cat for her symbolically, I'm certain, after Arwen, the elf prin-cess from Tolkein's *The Lord of the Rings* who waited in Rivendell for her beloved to rule before she could marry him. A dream, like many dreams that came to nothing in the waking world. I just liked the sound of the name – Arwen. A good word to roll on the tongue as you're learning to speak.

I held them all at bay as best I could aged two and three and four, demanding and receiving attention in equal measure, being taken for walks in the valley and learning the names of the flow-ers and the birds. My mother held many of them at bay just as earnestly, walking the valley in the quiet evening light, working in local schools or shooting off to record poetry for the BBC but always waiting for my father to conquer America or London, or wherever he was setting out his poetic stall that week, and come home to the valley. All I wanted from my father then was for him to be my first and best gruff billy goat as I lurked beneath the Roman bridge watching a sliver of summer sun slash through the water like laughter.

Books and songs and poetry were as important as landscape, as vital as breath. Freed from working on the land, I was taught to linger in it and take in every detail that I could. Farming was dying out, becoming broad and intensively agricultural in far-flung flatter lands than this, lands that didn't fold up like a fist – the fields below us were good for little but Melsome's cows and Captain George's sheep, which breached their fences with alarming regularity and came ambling through our gardens in a flurry of dung and hunger, looking for the choicest morsels the garden had to offer, flattening the tomatoes my father had raised, knocking over the towers of tyres in which we grew potatoes.

I was taught to delve into the landscape aesthetically rather than physically, so I learned to float into the names of flowers, lost in the beauty of cowslip and campion, dead nettle and Michaelmas daisy, beech tree and ash, but not much of immediate practical value was hard-pressed upon me. The valley was a palimpsest of imagination, of the living and the dead, and was accessible only through thought.

Occasional visitors would take us deeper into the landscape's confidence. John Cage came to visit us in the valley when I was very young and took us hunting after mushrooms, picking carefully through the clustering white skulls of fungus until he found something worth eating, which he brought back and cooked with what my father described as an intense care that produced four leathery fragments on a plate. I am fairly certain I refused to eat my share.

I was more interested in the sights and sounds of the valley, in imitating the birds and exclaiming excitedly about the pigs up at the sty attached to Sydenhams farm which my father held me up to see.

Mostly I remember walking in the harsh, exquisite summer light through the contrast between abbey-corseted lanes and fields that shimmered green as chameleons then vanished in a blaze of white. Nothing in between, no glum-clouded afternoons where all the greens of tree and field feel formulaic and even the campion fades from vibrant reddish pink to blackboard chalk simulacrum. Every morning was rosy in our little corner of the Slad Valley, and apples were abundant as dew.

Now the apple tree is gone, but for a bolt of knuckled wood that sinks into the landscape like Excalibur into a mossy stone. The soft lilacs of dwarf cyclamen are buried under scrub and all the Lords-and-Ladies have slithered off with their stems like sticky microphones to parties and pastures new. I am alone in the valley, with only words and memories to sustain me, and the echo of a song that hugs the tree line like a hunting owl.

2

Katy

I t was a wrench to leave behind birdsong, imagination, the gurgling lilt of water and my mother's undivided attentions and be a part of the wider world, but that was the price of growing older and surer of myself. Despite stubborn wailings and interminable attempts to make my mother stay in the valley with me, I was sent to nursery in Stroud whilst she worked as a supply teacher.

I did not take well to that separation. Nursery is built now only of vague memories: of parading on stage uncomfortably with a pillow stuffed up my jumper for some Christmas show whilst other, equally half-willing children teetered in and out of tune and half-learned lines; of refusing to sleep when the teacher insisted, wriggling on the floor as others napped or twitched, longing for butterflies and stickleback in the stream, not plastic cars and competition for attention. Of the few friends I made there, all but a couple of faces are now lost to time and indifference.

I learned, slowly, to separate the simple desires of valley life, where destiny was mine to play with and where I was part of everything, from the need to engage in less ecstatic realities. The valley was not mine alone for very long, anyway; I soon learned that there were other people who mattered just as much to the expanding landscape. Jean and Alan Lloyd lived above us in St Benedicts, a cottage originally as small as ours that had grown under Alan's craftsmanship into a long and eccentric house that would not look out of place on the Swiss Alps, were it not for the run of Cotswold stone that peeked out from behind the wooden cladding he had used to extended it. They produced a child, Katy, within a year of my appearance in the valley, a late arrival inspired, I'm told, by me.

By the time Katy could walk and talk, she had taken possession of the valley quite as much as I had, and had taken a leading role in my experience of it. The valley became ours largely because she said it must be so, because she insisted upon it with a stamp of her foot and a shriek if she was not listened to.

I was an only child, in need of the hurried urgency of sibling rivalry that she had learned from her two brothers, both ten or more years older than her, who teased and tortured and played mercilessly with her, daring her to take charge. She couldn't, so she took charge of me instead, leading our games with a shrill, amused insistence and a competitive streak that baffled and excited me to greater daring than my previously solitary existence had allowed.

Under Katy's tutelage, living in the valley became a delirious adventure. 'This is our house now,' cried Katy, pointing to a briar shrub where, in autumn, the best blackberries grew. The door was a tangle of branches and nettles. Tread hard enough and it would open – and we opened it often, only letting in Jake, the Lloyd's cheerful dog, whose eyesight was failing but who could find us every time with a snuffling devotion and who could not always be dissuaded from following us and becoming a damply affectionate part of our games. In the fields below my parents' cottage we could be ourselves, away from Jules and Jamie, who would only pin us to the sofa with enormous cushions and make us watch *Crossroads*, or refuse to switch over to *Doctor Who*, or accuse us with all seriousness of believing we were 'the bee's knees' if we let them near us. All we wanted was to be ourselves, free in a valley that no longer claimed them, because they were charging off with catapults or bows and arrows (which we secretly and desperately coveted) and friends, attempting to reclaim the valley or step over it into the mysterious outer reaches of a more grown-up life. Occasionally we would hear them shotgun-blasting their way through the woodland, taking potshots at pigeons and the occasional road sign or blaring through the green lanes on motorbikes, ignoring the bluebells and the wild garlic and roaring off in search of who knew what.

In those high summer moments of holiday and freedom, we barely noticed the parents who were never too far from us as we set off arguing, competing and adventuring, hand in hand, never quite sure who was in the lead yet never straying too far from home. We were always near enough to be heard if trouble came, though apart from a scraped knee or a nettle sting or a coat of mud from playing too hard amongst the exposed roots of trees by the stream, it never did.

We were deeply connected, in and out of each other's houses and always astonished if something prevented us from seeing each other. Once, when I was away on a day trip with my mother, leaving my father behind in the attic, writing, Katy came calling for me. When no answer could be got from knocking on the door, she was heard to yell though the letterbox, demanding I come out. She 'knew' I was in there, my father said, and was stridently determined to extract me whether I wanted to come out or not.

Bisley Bluecoat School was different, a separation I learned to enjoy, especially after Katy arrived there too, the year after me. I primped and paraded the learning I wallowed in at home at every opportunity, a bookish boy who outstripped his teaching aids and was reading the last book in the *Peter and Jane* series three years before he was supposed to, showing off for the teachers.

Mrs Lawty was my first teacher, but all I can remember of her now is the satisfied smile on her face when I showed her, with a swollen-headed excess of pride, my first wonky attempts at joined-up writing, not long after I had graduated to Mrs Swale's class. That, and the deep feeling of outrage at the news of her death, locked with my schoolmates inside the Terrapin classroom, as her body was carried to the graveyard that bordered the school in a procession we all wanted to be part of, though we did not know quite why.

School was activity and excitement, though of a more egalitarian sort than I was used to. Football in the tarmac yard, or cricket, at which the tomboyish Kim Mills excelled, leaping to catch the ball

above the wickets, rising high into the air, a determined grin on her face framed by a shock of black hair – the astonishment of the boys was vocal and intense. The shock of seeing Jamie Gibbons beaten by the Head in front of the whole school with a slipper for some affront I didn't understand or care about, the sort of punishment that was only ever dished out in the Beano or the Dandy and that just didn't happen at home.

I learned to adore people other than my mother at Bisley Bluecoats, too; a pretty young girl called Jane Millin caught my fancy aged seven and I was so enamoured of her that I named my pet mouse Jane in her honour. That fancy was brought to a crushing end when, at my eighth birthday party, Skanda Huggins told everyone who would listen exactly why I had a mouse called Jane, a wicked glint in his eye. I remember walking around the house distraught, the chill of betrayal cold as an owl's shadow hovering over me as the party spirit shivered and was stilled inside me.

That autumn, my father left the mouse house outside overnight, and Jane died in a sudden frost, as dead to me as I was to Jane Millin.

Getting to school was another adventure; with both parents working from home or away there was no regular bell to leave the house. It was up to me to move once I was out of the house and I was a dreamy child quite prepared to get lost in the hedgerows, watching the rabbits flit across the road in an angry, bobbing flash of white.

No matter that I was supposed to meet Katy at her house and walk up the hill with her to meet Doug, local postman and school-day cabbie, revving his homely chariot at the top of the steep hill at quarter to nine dead on – I still remembered the first day of school, the wrench of leaving the valley's apron strings and my mother behind to slip through the kissing gate into the beehive swarm of school; I trod ever so slowly up the hill.

Too easily distracted by springtime primroses or the venous scrabble of winter trees against the sky, I was always beaten to the taxi by Katy and only dragged out of my reveries by the hollow echo of a hooting car and Doug's amused and irritated cry of 'come on lightning'.

Katy, a small blonde avalanche rumbling with discontent in the back seat, would scowl at me, poke me in the ribs and roundly insult me for being a slowcoach all the way to school; a daily routine of dominance that we had invariably forgotten by first break. Unlike Rowena, the other passenger whom the car picked up first from Througham; she took it into her heart and head to maintain an antipathetic attitude towards my endless dreamy lateness that lingered far beyond playtime, unbroken but for the one time my school photos didn't come out and I was dragged from my maudlin state by her arm around my shoulder, hugging gently and shocking away the onset of tears.

When the snows came, so did adventure. The long crawl out of the valley to school – or work for my mother – often assisted by Norman Williams' tractor from Stancombe Farm, left us with choices. Being a village school, Bisley Bluecoats was open to all except the furthest flung, those who could not or would not escape their rural confines. Unless the snows cut the power off entirely, caved in the school's ceiling or simply came in a vengeful whirlwind and carried all the teachers away, we were expected to be there to learn, or understand at least that huddling together to keep warm was a fairly sure method of survival.

Sometimes the drifts swarmed higher than my head in a bid to shut us in – the lightning fork junction at the top of the hill where Doug the cab-driving postman would pick up Katy and, eventually, myself for school once drifted to six feet and didn't melt for weeks. We badgered our parents daily to be taken there to slide and climb and revel in the mountainous nature of the snow and it meant so much that to this day I'd still believe that Katy and I ventured up there every time entirely on our own, had she not in her possession parent-taken photos to prove otherwise.

My mother, on these snowy days, would pull out all the stops, bank up the fire and enter into a domestic frenzy in a bid to keep warm. The old house was tricky to heat – at least until the two-and-a-half-foot deep walls had soaked in enough warmth to begin radiating it back into the room. Once that had happened it felt like summer in the front room and springtime in the kitchen. The upstairs could feel like winter if we weren't careful with the night storage, but a tightly clutched hot-water bottle and a dash for bed was all the sport I needed to keep warm at night – sleep was only a rugby tackle away.

The house was soundtracked by 'Baby Love' or Peruvian flute music to keep us moving, whatever the weather. I can still smell the landscape around Slad when I hear certain records, wherever I am: Charlie Mingus's *The Black Saint and the Sinner Lady* evokes the stark and autumnal birdland we found walking in the woods, a dark mulch hiding bright wintry flashes of mushroom and sheep skull, the subtly shifting shadow towers of tree and a horn-scatter of pigeons; The Supremes' burst of morning sunshine – a spring day, bright as primroses; the haunting stream-song of *La Flute Indienne* cutting through a sticky summer; the all-encompassing *Abbey Road*, any time of year, anywhere, like the sun cutting through cloud, me with a nickel toffee hammer clutched in my hand, beating time to 'Maxwell's Silver Hammer' in the front room by the fire, or staring out of the bathroom window wondering which fast-flitting bird or deft squirrel darting along the low-slung yew might suddenly turn my way and put Sunday on the phone to Monday and Tuesday on the phone to me.

The house was all movement in winter days: the gentle shift of curtains when the draught excluder was out of place at the door and the fire was sucking in the cold, like an old man with a pipe, to stoke itself; the chatter from upstairs of my father's typewriter, his papers banked up around him like a frozen tidal wave of words, a staccato rhythm simmering under the music, following and dictating in the fire's percussion; me dancing in the wake of my mother as she shuffled through the routines of cooking, her mind on me, on other things, part of it quite somewhere else.

If it was too cold or bleak to go out walking, she would bend to the boredom and isolation of the winter by learning new things to make – the progress of the cheese soufflé she taught herself is deeply imprinted on me, starting out as a gooey but edible volcanic mess (edible, at least, if you are a devoted son who knows too well the effects of belt-tightening, even if you do not understand the causes) and eventually becoming an impossibly light, balloon-like explosion of taste that one had to be ready for when the oven door opened. We were invariably ready, my father and I, like a couple of greedy chicks opening their mouths wider than their bodies and clamouring for more, more, more.

These were only the inward, tiny winter adventures – my father would be away in London reading poetry, and sometimes my mother would have to cast off her domestic feathers and rise out of the snow to travel to Bristol to perform for the BBC. Suddenly the quiet domesticity of the valley would vanish and all would change, would become flowers. One memorable day, having scrambled through the snow to our car, parked far away at the top of the hills where the snow lay lighter, my mother paused at Stancombe's grass triangle junction, now a muddy white, and stared down the snow-bound fields marked out in kanji like a series of haiku.

'I'm going to be late,' she said, eyeing the slippery and barely troubled road. 'Or you are.' She looked at me, a half-smile on her mouth, guessing my answer before her question.

'Do you want to come to Bristol with me, or would you rather go to school?'

Out of the snow, out of school, off into the city. I remember watching her, silently, through the studio glass, bristling with the sense of a landscape in her voice as she recorded poetry for radio, the seed of a realisation that it mattered to listen, to take in the cadences of one's surroundings as much as the voices of the people, growing in my ear.

3

Three Points of the Diamond

I lived, then, in a small, enclosed galaxy, caught partly out of time between two villages, with few facilities but the ones we built for ourselves or the ones some long-evaporated glacier had gouged and melted into the valley millennia ago.

Electricity was a fairly new phenomenon in the valley – the mullioned cottage in which we lived, capped with a caul of yew, had only been wired up and connected to the water mains twenty or so years before we moved in. We were often travelling out, to Bisley, to Stroud and beyond, out of the enclosed sphere of the valley and into other worlds. We travelled less often to Slad, however; Slad was *us* and *other* at the same time, a smoke signal puff of civilization at the end of the valley. We could see it clearly from our garden, it was a mere two-mile stroll from our door, but the village always seemed far away.

It was due to the lack of a road in that direction, and the lack of a shop in Slad, the latter a change wrought in the wake of electricity and cars taking trade to larger villages and towns. Walking was for pleasure and escape; without the rattling, coughing second-hand car my mother had learned to drive whilst pregnant with me, we would have felt almost entirely divorced from the wider world.

We would strike out in Slad's direction often enough to visit Diana Lodge, the painter friend of my mother's, who was the first point on the erratic diamond of people who we knew in this valley before we came ourselves. Her house, Trillgate, was halfway to Slad and we would walk a quarter of a mile or more through mud and cowslips, avoiding horses and the occasional bull the farmer had forgotten to fence away from the footpath (which had once been the main road between Slad and Bisley) before we hit the tarmac, but we rarely walked on into the village itself.

Diana kept a caravan up in the Black Mountains, at Capel-y-ffin, just around the corner from the old monastery where Eric Gill had lived and worked, and where Gill's granddaughter and her family, the Davieses, still lived. My mother had met Diana there, visiting the old monastery with her mentor (and later my godfather) Father Brocard Sewell, a friend of Gill's in his youth. She became one of my mother's dearest friends.

A game and eccentric woman – she seemed to me to be built out of milk and mountains and to be as old and wise as the hills, though she was the same age as my grandmother – Diana had lived an extraordinarily full life. She married the poet Oliver W.F. Lodge in 1932, having initially answered his advertisement for a nude model, and had previously posed for Eric Gill and danced with the high-kicking Tiller Girls.

Diana and Oliver travelled, to Canada and the United States, gathering up a whorl of friends such as Lynn Chadwick and his first wife, the Canadian poet Ann Secord, who also found their way back to the area of Gloucestershire where Oliver had settled with his first wife, before her death, on the estate near Painswick of Detmar Blow, the Ruskin acolyte.

After Oliver's death, and after teetering on the verge of becoming a nun when her relationship with Leopold Kohr broke up, Diana embedded herself in Trillgate and into the landscape of Slad, becoming so much part of it that it seemed to me that she had never been anywhere else, despite painting the Black Mountains as well as the Slad Valley in an astonishing array of watercolours that captured the exactitudes of the landscape in a faintly surreal technicolour palate, and which she exhibited and sold in aid of charity until the end of her life.

Like her watercolours, Trillgate existed in a little bubble of faded Cotswold grandeur; a set of semi-modern kitchen units tacked on to the heart of an old, old house that ran you in circles if you walked through it and felt brave enough to walk through Diana's spartan bedroom and back down the worn stone semi-spiral of stairs that wound around the chimney stack. Kitchen and bedroom were very likely all there had been of the house once, and they were all that mattered of the house – as a child I ran through the chilly bedrooms and freezing drawing room, only stopping to hide in a tipped-up basket of an armchair next to the unlit fireplace, ready to leap out on unwary passers-by, or simply staring at the hugger-mugger collection of Diana's paintings, which filled the vast dining table and the nooks and crannies around it, but I did not linger in these rooms.

As with any good house, the only room that mattered when the garden was not available was the kitchen; its deep fireplace which housed a wood-burning stove and a defunct bread oven, its long wooden table with a high-backed pew running down the pantry wall that seated ten or fed forty if there were parties in the garden. The pantry itself was a thing of wonder, a walk-in cornucopia, lined with jar upon jar of preserves and foodstuffs that beggared the modest imaginings of a child raised in a small house that was always stocked but never replete.

Diana was a generous and warm woman – she welcomed and engaged with children as much as with adults, and my earliest memories of her are at Easter, when the garden became alive with hungry children engaged in her annual Easter egg hunt. We rushed back and forth amongst the exquisitely wild borders and through the small orchard hunting chocolate, as she stood by and laughed and encouraged us to look harder.

Diana was an intensely devout Catholic, having converted a few years before, but the only clue was in the subtle crucifix she wore and the quietly placed iconography in the kitchen – religion was never pronounced, never interfered with the joy and adventures of children, who ran roughshod and happy through the gardens as if they were theirs entirely to command, some little adjunct of Eden. The house itself was 'an act of worship in colour – [it] communicates joy similar to a Fra Angelico painting,' my mother wrote in a letter in 1969.

A sense of bohemia lingered like incense in Trillgate, more so when Diana's children and grandchildren came to visit. The eldest, Tom, brought over from Canada not only his three boys, Tom Jr., Lionel and Brodie, but a whiff of rock and roll glamour still clinging from his time on Radio Caroline, the pirate station of which he'd been the controller in the sixties. His brother Colin figured more in my life; a puckish man with a bright, jutting beard and a playful, quixotic demeanour, whose barking laugh chased us children wherever we ran throughout the house and garden.

His children, Owen and Caitlin, were regular visitors, up from Bristol. They came with a sharp, new manner, like a change in the air; the smell of the city on their breath. Owen played particularly hard, with a snap in his eye and a ready push that led to trouble and fun. Outside Diana's studio, a precarious log cabin built to be hidden just beyond the garden, I remember suddenly fighting back; inspired perhaps by Katy's years of more metaphorical pushing, I carried Owen over the edge of the veranda where he disappeared in an avalanche of nettle, bramble and boy, yelling and rolling down the hill to the fortuitous fence at the edge of the field. I remember the horror and the guilt of his fall, the way he slipped and rolled, the terror in the adults' eyes. I also remember the way Owen, bruised and scratched, got up laughing and groaning, and how nothing more was ever (nor ever needed to be) said.

It was a house of small, precise details hidden amongst the jumble of a bigger life: the Catholic icons stood out on the wall despite, or perhaps because of, their careful amalgamation into the general architectures of daily life. In the same way, Diana's intensively curated spirit filled her conversation, shaped by art and religion, by encounters with the great, the good and the not-so-good of the literary and artistic world, and by her piercing gentleness of thought and heart. By the full moon's light you could leave her house and walk deep into a Samuel Palmer painting as much because her conversation led you there as because the landscape around Slad was, and in places remains, akin to his visionary pastoral world.

The other direction in which we struck out was over the valley, down a scramble of path and over a ford in the stream before rising up and becoming suddenly enveloped by the trees of Keensgrove Wood. From there we followed the green lane through the skirts of Catswood, round through Redding Wood and out into the lane at the top of Elcombe to Rose Cottage. The woodland never seemed to cease, but there was a noticeable change along the mile or more that we walked – there was little traffic other than wild animals in the woods excepting the occasional stray sheep (or its remains, buried under bramble or wild garlic) and the occasional horse hoof-print, but the woods changed in their management.

Keensgrove was close and dark and low. The trees jostled for light and it was from here that the foxes and owls sounded most. Catswood opened out a little, made room for sweeping hides of bluebells or wild garlic enclosing the muscle and sinew of the hill, whilst Redding Wood opened out still further, its canopy sweeping up to the height of a cathedral before contracting suddenly into a narrow stretch of lane running parallel to the road; here, for many years, carefully hidden at the edge of the wood stood a red-and-black gypsy caravan that would have seemed gaudy had it been housed anywhere else. On closer inspection, it was as exquisite as a gingerbread house, with hooks for lanterns curving like talons over the steps and faded decorations by the door and on the panels at its side.

Brought up on Rupert annuals and the raggle-taggle gypsies-oh, I walked past this caravan half-expecting the name Rollo to be called and some apple-cheeked boy wearing a spotted scarf on his head to run up the lane to the caravan carrying a bundle of sticks or towing an unwilling and immeasurably large horse. I was always disappointed. Instead, beyond the tree line, there was Rose Cottage, a long house facing west and denied the sun by Swift's Hill, where there were different pleasures to be found; the next point on the rough-cut diamond of people and places we knew.

Rose Cottage was owned by John Papworth, who founded *Resurgence* magazine with Sir Herbert Read, E.F. Schumacher and Leopold Kohr (Diana Lodge's long-term partner after Oliver Lodge had died). Visiting there was often a strange experience, as John was a fierce and satirical man with all the fire of a preacher and the anarchic leanings of someone who had parted company with communism and the Labour party because of their authoritarian streak. He came across, in hindsight, as a peculiar, slightly alarming but more often than not delightful mix of John le Mesurier, Tony Benn and the Ancient Mariner.

Anyone and everyone who crossed his path was liable to be quizzed relentlessly by John, or at least by John's eyebrows, which seemed to be able to carry on conversations of their own, arching like a crow's wings up his forehead. He was a terror, a delight and a tease to children, prone to giving vent to opinions that confounded many of them, not least myself, and bringing religion into the conversation at unexpected angles. He would often look at me sternly and announce that 'Adam was a gardener!' fixing me, as an eagle might a rabbit, with an eye glowering out from beneath one arched eyebrow before quickly bounding off on another, possibly related but considerably less alarming, topic.

Given that my only attempts at gardening tended to amount to little more than chasing my father down our long, narrow garden with a hosepipe through stacked tyre potato beds and picking the apple mint and lemon balm that grew like weeds outside our front door, I took a little fright at this pronouncement at first, sure that he had seen something or knew something that I didn't. Whether that was the case or not, the fright wore off with repetition (anyway, I was going to be a fireman, or an acrobat – never a gardener).

The final point on the diamond was Laurie Lee, whom we visited less often, more often than not in his lesser-known drinking haunt, The Star, which as far as I can tell was used for quieter conversations, conversations that scratched under the surface of his public persona, a place no tourist knew or dared to enter.

The Woolpack was always for public Laurie, impish and amusing Laurie who knew very well the wider impact of *Cider with Rosie*, for the Laurie who would encounter tourists and tease them. One encounter outside the Woolpack ran as follows:[1] a tourist, most probably American and certainly immensely swayed by Laurie's description of village life, so much so as to believe it took place millennia ago in a lost world more akin to Tolkien's Shire than the actual reality, stumbled down, awed, to the Woolpack's door out of the steep and tree-lined churchyard set into the bank opposite the pub. Puffed out and tired from a search around the precarious gravestones, which permanently teeter on the edge of falling like an old boxer's teeth, the tourist stopped a smartly dressed older gentleman in a white fedora, who was making his way home from the pub, and asked: 'Excuse me, could you tell me where Laurie Lee is buried?'

Laurie looked at the tourist wryly and, in warmly arch tones, announced: 'I don't know about up there, but if you come in to the pub later you'll find him buried in a pint.'

My first memories of Laurie are not of him buried in a pint, however, but of him buried in conversation. I'm not suggesting that pints weren't involved, just that all that I remember from these meetings of poets at The Star was the way the drive up to the pub, now a private house halfway between Slad and the Vatch, rose from the road in an elegant tarmacadam sweep; how the trees obscured the valley from sight; how bird and sunlight created an erratic and ever-changing shadow play of sheet music; how intensely my parents, my mother in particular, talked with Laurie about poetry and landscape and the valley we all shared; and how little I would interrupt, caught between the dark and attractive sense-scape of the pub, the conversation and the sun reaching back to ruffle the scalp of Swift's Hill.

From a very early age I had a sense of Laurie being buried in this valley, alive and breathing yet thoroughly rooted in, a spirit of mischief and nature and place. Not that I would have put it like that then, but that is the sensation that has grown out of every childhood encounter with him, and as often as he might shoot off to London dressed in his public suit there was no doubt that something of him always lingered here.

---

1 This is the version that has done the rounds since Laurie's death. His original telling of it involved two schoolgirls and came in a clean and a bawdy version. Like all good stories, the telling of it has mutated bit by bit over the years.

The sense that, locally, a pint was raised to Laurie's success only to be followed by the occasional sour whiskey chaser to 'too-much-success-for-a-local-boy-done-a-bit-too-good-and-he-knew-it' has only confirmed this. I was part of the new breed of incomers whose arrival brought continual changes to the valley, changes that have slowly set it ever further apart from the supposed halcyon of *Cider with Rosie*. As an outsider, granted access but still only looking in as from a distance, my roots set raw and loose in Slad soil, I grew up celebrating Laurie's vision of a distant land that still crumbled gently underfoot.

4

Religion, Sex and Chickens

Religion grows with shallow roots in valleys like Slad, where children can run off into the woods and make their own churches. It's the adults that keep it going, keep on trying to throw more mulch in to deepen it in their children and settle the roots.

We maintained a regard for all the morbid fascinations of funerals and the darker, stranger dealings of Genesis, but Katy and I had little time for the formal expressions of it, however much our parents may or may not have wanted us to learn to love Sunday School. Certainly we fought for parts in the school Nativity – I was always the narrator and I seem to recall that Katy was a reluctant shepherd with ambitions at Mary – but when it came to the Sunday morning agonies, we accepted with bad grace.

Fortunately, our agonies were brought to an abrupt end – the last time I can remember going to Sunday School, we were dropped off by the gate that led through the schoolyard to Bisley church and waved to as we stomped like churls across the tarmac yard. Arriving at the church I tried the door. It would not open. Katy knocked. There was no answer. We knocked a couple more times before one of us (Katy, I suspect) decided that we should check if parents were still there. They weren't.

Nothing happened in the churchyard. It was a hazy spring morning and we knew that flowers were opening in the valley, the tree line was beginning to obscure the sky with green. We would rather have been there. Yet here we were, stuck in a shrouded churchyard on our own with nobody coming. There was no Sunday School that day.

Irritated, we amused ourselves, chattering away with our backs against the cool grey gravestones or climbing on the tombs. We didn't stray far, certain that at some point someone would come, either the Sunday School or parents or both. Nobody passed by – only the cautious buzzing of insects and the distant rush of the village wells was audible under our voices.

Somebody must have seen us there, playing quietly, and recognised us, called the valley in the hope that someone would be home. They must have got the party line because it was our neighbour John Horton who came to take us away.

John and Judy Horton had taken over the Old Chapel at the end of our garden in 1975, bringing with them a sense of wildness and other-worldliness that moved the chapel farther away from its roots. Instead of religious musical murmurings emanating from the chapel, the air on a Saturday night was filled with smoke-fuelled, husky versions of Bob Dylan songs. To this day I find it impossible to listen to *Street Legal* without thinking of the Hortons and their visiting friends, who all seemed to have wildly improbable and exciting names like Spike, wailing and strumming away at the songs. I remain firmly of the opinion that their stripped back versions were better than the actual album. They were a joyously anarchic family to be around.

Judy, a wiry Australian woman, was gloriously impatient with my tendency to wail louder after an accident if I knew my mother was on her way and immensely brusque with me when I reacted in very vocal horror to the fish head soup she was cooking (my mother had had a Linda McCartney moment in the mid-1960s having seen lambs playing in a field and vowed never to eat meat again – I was as a consequence brought up vegetarian, putting me immediately at odds with the country children at school), dismissing my objections with a pithy put-down and a sharp reminder that it wasn't for me.

John, who had rebuilt the chapel whilst they lived at Driftcombe, the big, grand, cold place at the other end of the valley, I remember as an altogether more laid-back individual (unless the car broke down – I recall being pulled in hasty panic to the Midland Bank building in Cheltenham as John's car erupted in smoke by the side of the road) who led the games that inevitably started with Jessie and Luke, their two children.

Luke was too young to figure much in my valley life, except as an inevitable wailing presence, but Jessie, a year or so younger than Katy, became an integral part of the gang that Katy and I had formed in the absence of other gangs. Jessie was anarchy personified as a four- and five-year-old – climbing up to the tree house in the yew beside Katy's house, in which both girls were already roosting, I said something that clearly annoyed them both. 'Stop him coming up here,' cried Katy. Jessie hoisted up her skirt and peed on me. I jumped and ran, too surprised to even complain.

We were perpetually in and out of each other's houses from then on, the three of us, a small community re-naturing the way the valley and its contents worked. We explored down the lane to Mrs Bevan's old cottage, thrilling at its quietness and emptiness and to the stories of a family of wild cats that had once been her brood; walked past it to Driftcombe to climb an easy, slanting yew. Driftcombe, at the end of the valley, was owned by Duncan Smith and let to holidaymakers in the summer and to six-monthly tenants in the winter. It was so near the point of the valley, beneath steep hills, that even though it was south-facing it got next to no sun at midwinter. Unlike Mrs Bevan's strange little derelict house, which seemed to be merely empty, a place fraught with everyday dangers in which we refrained from playing, Driftcombe was reputedly haunted. We did not go near on our own except in daylight, as visitors when people were about, with parents.

Not going near the house was one thing, but its pond was far enough away to investigate, rife as it was with water boatmen, skating in aerobic languor across the water's tensile surface, and dragonflies diving through supine willow branches. Unlike the stream at the other end of the valley, it was ideal to push wooden boats out on, and all weary sailors come summer liked gooseberries fresh from the prickly bush a couple of yards away.

Above the looming shadow of Driftcombe, up into the rough, untended woodland, we found shells of houses to investigate, the skeletal debris of a valley that had once been much more heavily populated, which had boasted its own pub and the main road from Slad to Bisley cutting up through it. We knew nothing of this then, making house in the toothy remains of others' homes one hundred and more years after they had gone, walking in their footsteps and never knowing that we were more like ghosts than any spirit, imagined or otherwise, that haunted the big house below us.

As we grew older, the presence of neighbours became more pronounced; the Wildes moved into the cottage in the middle of our terrace and took what had been an incoherent grassy space beyond their front door and tamed it to patio in direct contravention of their surname. At first they were there rarely, as work was underway. In their absence, Katy and I colonised their patio for more formal games. One favourite was King of the Castle, which involved shouting at each other and waving sticks while swaying precariously on the high, sharp wall that offered a pleasingly sheer drop into a little hedged-off suntrap ten feet below and headily close access to a spot which the local adders had chosen as a basking point as soon as the stones were laid.

Another was Grandmother's Footsteps, in which my father – already an excellent and much-practised Billy Goat Gruff down at the stream – excelled as the wolf.

'What's the time, Mr Wolf?' we called, creeping slowly up behind him.

'12.15 and 32 seconds,' he replied. We crept a little closer.

'What's the time, Mr Wolf?' we yelled again in ragged chorus.

'LUNCHTIME!'

We froze unsteadily as he span around, revealing a wicked glint in his eye, his beard exploding into view like a dust-storm cloud in negative, black and brown, red-streaked and wolfish.

'I can see your washing-tub face quivering,' he growled, pointing at Katy.

Katy, entirely unable to resist a taunt, and especially that one, set her face to a frown and her shoulders forward.

'I have NOT got a washing-tub face,' she said, sourly.

'You moved!' I said, exultant.

'So did you,' she said, in a huff of high-pitched exasperation.

'You're both lunch,' yelled my father and chased us home.

They were anything but wild, the Wildes; a pleasant enough urbanite couple with enough money to take a weekend cottage in the country. They were endlessly fascinating to me, and to my friends, not because they were particularly approachable or fun for a child to be around, but because they would bring out a jar of sweets if they saw children passing and hand them out in genial fashion, as if bribing their way in to the local scenery.

Because I lived next door, I was best placed to profit from this generosity. With a careful eye for their exits into the daylight I wandered past with a winning smile every time I saw an opportunity. Then one weekend Skanda Huggins came to stay, and was offered a sweet as well. Prone, in tandem, to conjuring up very reasonable-seeming sorts of mischief (in our eyes at least), Skanda and I immediately started planning a campaign of extraction that would, we were certain, have made any military leader proud. We staked out the Wilde's patio and whenever the doorway twitched, came sweeping past in the flush of some instantly invented and entirely see-through 'game', designed to carry us past their door as they came out and guarantee us sweets – mints and penny chews, strawberry bonbons, anything sugary that would last a while without going off in a damp old Cotswold stone weekend cottage.

They cottoned on to our routine quite quickly and laughed at us, assuming it was little more than a passing phase. They were childless. They had no idea of the tenacious hold that sugar had on the minds of children who are afforded ten pence to spend on sweets in the village store every Saturday, but only if they're very good. Even in 1978, ten pence didn't go particularly far, when there was the lure of Space Dust and Spangles and Mars Bars and Blackjacks and so much more – the kilner jar full of sweets we knew to be lurking on the shelf in their front room, and which surely by now had our names engraved upon it, was too much temptation. So, when Skanda came again, we upped the stakes.

We were children. We didn't think beyond the rush of sugar in our blood. We didn't understand completely that they came down to the valley for peace and quiet, to escape the giddy rush of London. Anyway, the valley was mine, and by extension Skanda's, because he was with me and together we were impish and trouble – boys, in other words. Even Katy wouldn't always get a look in when Skanda was around.

Derek and Margaret Wilde tolerated our second campaign, but their suburban veneer wore a little thin by the end of the weekend, as they didn't get more than a few minutes peace to themselves outside. At the third campaign, a few weeks later, they retired indoors for much of the weekend. We could hear them moving around inside, through the thin skin of brick that separated the two houses. Eventually there was a measure of silence.

'They've gone outside,' said Skanda, excited.

'Let's go and have a look,' said I.

'What are you going to have?' said Skanda, pulling on his boots.

'I think I'd like a blackjack,' I replied, wrestling with my jumper. 'What about you?'

We didn't wait for what Skanda wanted, but barked a brief good-bye to my mother in the kitchen and ran next door. Nobody was in the garden. We looked, puzzled. We'd been too quick for them to have strayed too far away from their house.

'Is their car still there?' I said.

We ran up to the lane. Their car was still there, perched inside a green tin garage, built in a gaudy and poor attempt to blend with its surroundings. We ran back to the house.

'Why don't we knock?' said Skanda.

'Yes, let's,' I said.

We knocked. There was no answer. We knocked again, louder, then stood back on the patio staring up at the small windows above us; still no reply. We knocked a third time, as loud as both our small pairs of fists could manage. There was an eruption in the sky, like a badger falling through the branches of a tree, and harsh language muffled by Cotswold stone.

A moment later the front door opened, and Derek stood there, half-dressed, his appearance finally torn away from 'smart Londoner come to the country' and living up gloriously to his surname.

'What the hell do you want?' he roared.

We blanched.

'We ... we wondered if we could have a ... sweet?' I murmured, looking to Skanda for support.

'Um ...' said Skanda.

'Go home and don't come asking for any f***ing sweets any f***ing more,' roared Derek. 'We would like some f***ing peace and quiet.'

We fled, clattering like pigeons through the gate and stood, shaking, in the kitchen. I think my mother laughed. She may have offered us Tigger Juice, a concoction of her own invention blending milk, spice and honey. She certainly didn't offer us any support once she'd worked out what we'd interrupted.

I remember family visits as exotic visitations. My mother's sister Olive came most often, with her husband Alan and their children Graham and Zoë. Pleasingly conventional, thoroughly English, they were no less exotic for all that, since they did not live close by. The arrival of my father's family was eye-openingly strange, however; a collection of Jews from all over the world trooping down the path looking decidedly different: Aunt Judy, with hair almost as red as mine, over from Israel with Aunt Gustel; Aunt Elise from Paris with her half-Vietnamese children Daniel and Olivia; Aunt Selma and Uncle Alfred over from California with their daughters Wendy and Roberta; cousins David and Miriam from London; and at the head of the line my Grandmother, Rosi, a tiny, calm and beautiful woman as compact and lined as a walnut, wearing a blue headscarf and a seraphic smile.

The valley came alive with a multitude of accents and new ideas, religious imperatives outweighed by familial bond. These visits were quite a breakthrough. My father, the rebellious youngest, had 'married out' of a very orthodox family and 'run off' to be a poet to considerable disapproval (my Aunt Elise had also 'married out' – a rebel figure in the family since childhood, she had encouraged my father in his upheavals against the conventional regimentations of Orthodox Judaism). Only after I was born did my Grandmother relent, and come to visit us. The pull of grandchildren is at least as powerful as prayer. The house was made spick and span and as kosher as it was possible for *goyim* to manage, my mother being at pains to make the religious as welcome as those who cared little for the faith.

Even so, my father would add devilment to the occasion, keeping ham in the house even though he knew that his mother was coming. He would stand with his back to the kitchen sink, slipping morsels of dead pig into his mouth secretly. He only stopped when I asked 'Why are you eating dead pig?' in a loud voice, unaware of the religious implications and only concerned for the poor pig, whose compatriot I stared at over the wall whenever we passed Sydenhams Farm. I am sure there was suppressed laughter from some of the family, and a mildly disappointed look in my Grandmother's kind eyes. I remember that look because it was such a rare occurrence on her face; normally all she projected was love and the comfort of knowing that, despite being born away from her faith, I was her grandson. There was a certain pleasure, too, in the fact that, because I was vegetarian, I was kosher by default.

We kept a brood of bantams for a few years, in a haphazard run built halfway down the garden, which we shifted once or twice to keep the earth scratched clean of weeds, before we sold them on. My father, out of the attic and in puckish, bucolic mood, would dance past them singing their names in a chorus of increasingly jazzy melodic lunacy and scattering feed through the chicken wire before he went to tend the vegetables farther down the garden.

They were a capricious lot, these birds, forever fighting for dominance in the small run and eager to escape and loiter through the vegetable patch we shared with the Hortons, daring the local foxes into action. A couple at least were lost to the fox, slicing his way under the wire at night and causing havoc, but not before they had made their mark on me.

We got them when I was six, and all I could dream about was chickens – Arwen got some respite from my attentions for a while.

Aged three I had driven off her son, Baggins, thanks to my tender ministrations to his tail. I remember poor Baggins levitating round the kitchen in his desperation to escape me, knocking pots from the shelves and yowling. He was last seen, wild eyed, disappearing into the throng of feral cats round Mrs Bevan's derelict cottage from where, my mother was certain, half his seed had come. I was kinder to Arwen – my mother made sure of that, leaning in to tell me, gently but firmly, when I went too far – and by the time the bantams came along, my desire to interact with animals was tempered with a measure of restraint.

Restraint was no dam for fascination, however, and every morning I went hunting through the roosts for eggs, carefully unlatching and pulling back the flaps on the side of the hut and watching as the outraged bantam shuffled away from her warm straw onto the shit-streaked walkway, a feisty bicker dying slowly in her throat. When she had retreated far enough, in went my fingers with a lover's delicacy, sifting the straw for the warm, speckled oval, which I then reverently deposited in my mother's apron pocket. Every day came new rewards for my delicacy until, on my seventh birthday, we found seven perfect eggs, all of them different, slipped them out of the straw in trembling fingers, as warm in my hand as if they were alive. Better than cakes or candles; a feast, a miracle. The valley and the chickens loved me.

That sensation of reciprocated love lasted until Christmas, when my cousin Zoë came to stay. Zoë was not a vegetarian and my Aunt Olive, packing her off for Christmas to her bohemian, vegetarian sister's house, could not envisage that she'd survive the festivities without the requisite roast, so in a Tupperware came a chicken ready-roasted for the feasting.

It was a huge amount of chicken – far more than Zoë could eat and bigger even than the eyes and stomach of my father, who happily and regularly put cooked meats from Stroud and London delis into the fridge, emitting loud yumming sounds when he took them out again. Christmas passed, as Christmas usually does, in a haze of food and music and games and laughter, but at the end a large part of the chicken carcass remained. We didn't know what to do with it, and didn't want to waste it, but all the neighbours were either away or replete.

So, ceremoniously and without consideration for the consequences, we marched the chicken corpse down the garden to the bantam run and threw it into the wire coop. There was an explosion in the hen run; bantams came booming from the hatch in a storm cloud of feather, battling to get to the new arrival. Oozo, the scruffiest and most determined of our hens, a black and white speckled tartar who didn't so much rule the roost as run it with a neo-fascist efficiency, doling out pecks and beatings to any hen fool enough to stand in her way, pounced upon the corpse. She lifted it up with a mad little gleam in her eye, waving it about triumphantly. And then all hell broke loose. Anarchy reigned in the chicken coop. Oozo's supremacy fell to pieces as all the other hens bombarded her for a share of her cannibal prize.

We watched, a sense of horror smothering us like mist, astonished at the frenzy, as feathers were torn out and blood was drawn as they fought each other for a taste of flesh; at how, within minutes, the chicken corpse had been reduced nearly to bone, split apart and quartered around the coop by hens pecking out a manic rhythm and clucking at each other in fury if their personal circles of attrition were invaded as they hacked the last scrap from their distant kin.

I wasn't quite so keen on eggs or chickens after that.

5

Beat

Like many writers, my mother collected her ideas whilst walking, often on the edge of night, in a state of concentrated thoughtfulness and forgetfulness, striking out into the woods, on her own or with friends.

The valley was sometimes a cage around which she prowled. We had moved there because she did not want to bring me up in the city she had hated, had wanted a place of peace and escape, somewhere to retreat to away from the urban bubble and toil. My father, however, was still deeply embroiled in London, and was there regularly, leaving us alone in the woods, in the dark. Though he was, of course, attempting to 'bring home the bacon', the tight nuclear unit that she had envisaged was stressed and strained by his long tours and engagements. She kept house in the meantime, travelled to Bristol or London for readings and recordings for the BBC when she could, filling up the low times between engagements with supply work in local schools, waiting for the times of plenty when my father returned.

She instinctively, intellectually slipped the bars of the cage on these walks out into the half-light of the valley, looking for the bones of its myths and histories whilst I was looked after by Jean and Alan

Lloyd or the Hortons, playing with Katy and Jessie or reading books, knowing nothing of her loneliness yet only too glad to see her when she returned. Isolation, as for many poets, was a necessity for her pen and spirit, and she took full advantage of it, though after a while it could chafe and burn.

What ghosts or gods she found slipping through mud on the dark path through Keensgrove Woods only her poems can tell and they are often potently elusive. Poems such as 'Letter to be sent by air' however, written to my father on a trip to America, are at least in part an expression of her occasional sense of dislocation and loss within the valley, for all that '... the child shouts at the sky/declares its portents'.

> sometimes my head is a lightness
> filled with dry grass
> I spread into the sky
> over seas and wide forests
> to find you
> how you are torn out of me
> a cry not my own splits the wind
> I am streaming with air
> where are your limbs in this whiteness?
>
> in the night intervals
> as speech to the tongue
> I am near to you
>
> as blood to the earth
> I conjure you home

To me the valley was consumed with light, as I was with her. When my father was there too, the house and the trees and the whole valley full of birds and creatures sang to the tune of their voices. Yet it is her voice that I remember most clearly from childhood, which comes back to me decades later, long before her face. As John Papworth put it:

... that voice – gentle, faintly husky, full of warmth and friendliness, and roseate with the most exquisitely delicate articulation and modulation ... It sometimes seemed to me her very soul was in her voice, even when she conversed on mundane things.

She once read to me from her poetry in her Cotswold cottage and some of the lines, coupled with the luminously distinctive sound of her voice, echoed within and uplifted me for days; but I noticed that at public readings she had that same capacity quietly to rivet an audience and to transmute its attention into a silent sense of almost Elysian ecstasy.

As a young boy, almost all I ever craved in the quiet moments when I was not running through the valley, convinced that I was in charge of its light and growth and of the direction the earth span, was that voice, that attention, the ecstatic calmness that it instilled in me, whether she was reading me stories, or poems, or encouraging me to do the same.

I would walk in her wake in deep attachment, a jealous little copper-headed blur of admiration. When she directed the mummers play one Christmas (the worthies of Bisley revelling in the fact that they had a RADA-trained actress to bring the show back to life) I, although playing the Doctor, learned every part by heart because, though I really wanted to be Saint George, I was ready to do anything for the show and wanted to impress upon my mother that there was nothing that I could not do. I remember dancing on the sidelines, waiting my turn to speak, in the cold main street of Bisley, outside the old gaol, my back to its heavy, barred and lidless eyes, breathing out Saint George's lines in clouds of shivering steam.

I learned poetry by rote with her as well (not because she insisted, but because it was natural to do so) and learned to listen to the cadences and rhymes of the poetry she rehearsed for shows she toured with Robert Gittings celebrating Hardy and Keats, listening out with an eager ear for new sounds and meanings. Often the valley answered us back, reinforcing poetry that was being read aloud with interpolations of its own.

Charles Causley was a particular favourite of mine – his collection of poems for children, *Figgie Hobbin*, was stuffed with memorable characters such as Colonel Fazackerly Butterworth-Toast and vicars who didn't recognise their own daughters, all of whom were dressed in the most delicate mnemonics of rhythm and rhyme.

One Causely poem that particularly stuck in my head, and delighted me enough to wake my parents one Sunday morning, leaping on their bed and demanding they listen to me read, was 'I Saw a Jolly Hunter', a bouncingly gleeful poem about a hunter out after a hare. The Jolly Hunter shoots himself dead by accident whilst the Jolly Hare gets away; the perfect poem for a vengeful seven-year-old vegetarian who instinctively requires the animal to survive at the expense of the hunter.

I launched into the poem as my parents blearily sat up in bed, enunciating every word in punctilious imitation of my mother and, at the exact moment I read the line *Bang! went the jolly gun*, a shotgun gave its retort deep in the woods, echoing through the closing lines of the poem:

Hunter jolly dead
Jolly hare got clean away.
Jolly good I said.

'Jolly good!' said my father, bounding up from under the covers in naked refugee sympathy for the escaping underdog, meat eater though he was.

'The valley's listening,' said my mother.

Later, quietly, I hoped that it had not been listening too hard and consumed one of the Lloyds as they stalked through the woods for pigeons with their shotguns.

Those early, unshorn days of my childhood were as perfect as my mother could make them. Free of London, she threw her all into writing, teaching and keeping me occupied. We were just about comfortable – poets tend to swing through life on the breadline, leaping occasionally up into the baker's window when a commission or a reading comes in – but much time and money was put into the paperwork that surged like a sea through the attic, letters and poems and paintings for my father's endless un-commercial but extraordinarily richly textured countercultural magazines. My mother battled continually to stem the tide of paperwork at the attic stairs.

The front door welcomed one into a cosy little corridor lined with books and coats and boots and binoculars. The kitchen, to the left, was a cork-tiled haven – a narrow, yellow-walled galley filled with flowers and bits of pottery she had carefully accrued, plus a long pine table that filled one end of the room and looked out into the sunset, westwards to Slad through a pair of Liberty print curtains that drew together like a tangle of flowers. Arwen would lurk behind them, staring in at us with one green eye, the other hidden by Liberty.

The front room was all bare stone and books, shelves of them covering the thin brick wall dividing the houses as a feeble but beautiful insulation against travelling sound. She sourced everything carefully and locally – the rocking chairs in which I careered dangerously were from local makers, the hard green utilitarian carpet that left indentations in my knees if I knelt too long on it was from a shop in Stroud, there were rough-hewn benches and a painting of flowers she'd made when she was seventeen. In amongst this she placed the treasures she found in the woods. A sheep skull she'd found and written about took pride of place on the mantelpiece, alongside a delicate glass vase that was as violently yellow as a varnished egg yolk.

Upstairs, a cool, clean bathroom, a separate lavatory and two bedrooms. Mine was narrow and yellow and covered with posters of Breughel and of lions and unicorns dancing attendance to medieval ladies in wimples. Luminous stars glowed between the black beams at night. My parents' room was green, with a map of the valley on one wall and a fool asleep on a hill opposite. The floorboards were painted black. Above this, the attic, in which one could sometimes find a box of crisps, a television or my father, if the tides were right, chattering away at the typewriter one-fingered, a green eyeshade of the sort worn by newsmen and card-sharps in films from the 1940s propped on his brow.

There was always a sense of shifting in the attic, the papers ebbing and flowing around the big Buddha chair from which

I watched television on rare occasions. It was my father's place, his rickety sanctuary, where he sometimes hid if visitors came. At night he would work on the kitchen table, but always before breakfast the papers were hurried upstairs and locked back behind my mother's barrier of clean.

'I hear you call my head a bin/where children dip their buckets in,' my father would sing to her when she was down, bringing up a bubble of laughter in her throat. I envied his ability to make her laugh and tried to emulate it. She encouraged more seriousness in me, steered me towards careful writing, reading and speaking aloud.

In her lonelier periods in the valley, when my father was away, she took me walking, learning the names of flowers and the birds. I sucked in the knowledge, writing little poems about sheep in the fields and red campion and autumn. In 'Poem of Absence', she wrote:

> to be alone for a month is good
> I follow the bright fish of memory
> falling deeper into myself
> to the endless present
> the child's cry is my only clock

Yet the years wore on and my father's absences became longer – sometimes I found him at Stroud station, suddenly beardless after a long trip around North America and didn't recognise him. I hid behind my mother's legs, shy and scared.

> I sit in the woods at dusk
> listening for the sound of your singing
> there are letters from a thousand miles
> you wrote a week ago
> like leaves from an autumn tree
> they fall on the mat
>
> it was your voice woke me
> and the absent touch of your hand

Absence stilled her, made her harder to reach. She would range out into the night on longer walks and take holidays to Cornwall with me only. Men would come to the valley, bringing parcels of adoration that she would not open, or at least not when I was there. I remember some of them vividly, the flash of their hopeful faces bright in the window, the way they were delicately attendant to my needs, solicitous and courtly and absolutely not welcome because they were distractions from my real business of living.

I only remember a couple of these interlopers and admirers fondly. Oswald Jones, a balding Welsh photographer, one of her dearest friends, who loved her deeply and took ceaseless photos of her (all of which she archly dismissed as awful), used to snarl at, satirise and tease me till I was his devoted friend. 'Old Oz' she called him, keeping him carefully, delicately at arm's length. We had a little wooden begging bowl with a face on its handle that looked like Ossie, which my mother used for raisins, perhaps as a jest at his fondness for alcohol. I remember the quietly mortified look on his face when I gleefully told him it was called the Ossie bowl.

Then there was Roger Garfitt, a lithe and cautious poet in his mid thirties who came one day in March 1980 for a visit that lasted a fortnight and made a huge impression on me. In part it was the fact that he looked like Dick Turpin, as played by Richard O'Sullivan on the TV on Saturday afternoons – the only thing that was guaranteed to keep me indoors and which infested my imagination in numerous games around the valley and was reported as outright fact in my Monday morning news book at school. I remember arguing with Katy that she had to be Turpin's partner, Swiftnick, because she had the right colour hair. She was having none of it. Both of us wanted to be Turpin.

Roger was an exotic curiosity, parked on the divan downstairs every morning for two weeks. To my mind, he wrested any claim I might have had on being Dick Turpin, and was exciting company for it. I went to school content that there was something new and interesting to come home to, blissfully unaware that my mother was not keeping Roger at arm's length as soon as I had marched up the hill to the cheerful yell of 'Come on lightning'.

It was not just the fact that he resembled the heavily romanticised TV Turpin, who in imagination had accompanied me through every nook and cranny of the valley, upsetting imaginary apple carts and buckling bucket-loads of swash to every tree. As much as anything it was my mother's excitement rubbing off on me, an emotion that had been lacking in her for more than a year.

Before long we were heading off to visit her oldest friend Jane Percival with him whilst my father was away on another American tour. It came as only a small surprise to me when my mother and I packed ourselves into a bright orange Peugeot and left the valley for Sunderland, to live with him.

It had been a long time coming, not that I knew it in my territorial, devotional state of being, certain that I was the only thing that mattered to her. My father was away too often, of necessity most of the time, earning money, but also finding distraction in the wider world. Though he devoted vast and eccentric energies to the maintenance of the life we shared, he was fundamentally more urban than my mother, who had always been less temperamentally attuned to the streets of cities and the hustle and bustle of arts communities and literary worlds.

The valley was a place of haven for him, of peace and familial contentment, when he was there. But my mother, whether in her country camouflage of black padded coat and a broad rimmed floppy hat or peering through elderflowers with a wry, seductive grin on her face, her stark outer beauty softened by childbirth and need, still found it hard to be so often in the valley without him. A fragility crept in more often under her upturned smile, beneath the faintly medieval clothes she wore, her tapestry of greens, blacks, browns and muted blues, past the tiny bouquets of flowers she plucked from wood and hedgerow to adorn the kitchen table. The dreams of food for free, her son brought up away from pollution and the screech of competition, the search for contentment out of the hubbub of the city, had come at a cost; a partial disquiet of the soul. Intact, our family operated in a fizzing whorl of joy; with just a few neighbours and myself for company, solitude was sometimes difficult for her to bear.

In the book she wrote during the ten years we lived there, *Water Over Stone*, a marked sorrow and a noticeable edge of fear creeps into her writing, inevitable perhaps after entry into her middle years and the death of her father, with whom she had had a difficult relationship. In 'Walking in Autumn', dedicated to Diana Lodge, with whom she shared much in common excepting Diana's ability to be wholly solitary, at once at one with the landscape and apart from it, she writes about the walk to Elcombe along the green lanes through Keensgrove wood, about how darkness falls and the walkers experience a sudden onrush of fear:

> We hurry without reason
> stumbling over roots and stones.
> A night creature lurches, cries out,
> crashes through brambles.
> Skin shrinks inside our clothes;
> almost we run
> falling through darkness to the wood's end,
> the gate into the sloping field.
> Home is lights and woodsmoke, voices –
> and, our breath caught, not trembling now,
> a strange reluctance to enter within doors.

In hindsight this fragility, this fear to enter within doors seems to me to mark the point at which she needed to move on, to escape the quiet of the valley. She was sinking into the landscape rather, without someone to help her rise above it, to share its mysteries with, bone and water and stone becoming less a balm against the prescriptive rigours of day-to-day existence, supply teaching in schools, touring shows and recording for the BBC than it once had been.

My father, despite his itinerant lifestyle and his long absences from the valley, could not and would not let her go without a valiant effort to make her change her mind. Like Lord Lovelace in Charles Causley's poem from *Figgie Hobbin*, he came charging back '... whistling bright as any bird/Upon an April tree', bringing with him guests and entreaties and all the love that he could muster. His hopes were dashed.

Amongst these guests was Allen Ginsberg who, in the company of his partner Peter Orlovsky and the poet Tom Pickard, came to visit in 1979, a year before my mother and I left. They came on a wet

November night, down the precarious hill to the cottage, bringing an exotic whiff of excitement in their wake.

A reading had been arranged in Stroud on Bonfire Night, behind Starters café where my parents would take me for a treat after shopping trips to town. (I can still feel the indignant thrill that shivered through me when my father snuck a can of Guinness out of his bag in Starters and filled up his glass, which had briefly contained cola before he tipped it away; the terror that we might be caught.) But before this came our gathering of poets in the woods, with my mother carefully cooking exquisite food, and peals of laughter at jokes that leapt over my head like proverbial cows orbiting the moon.

Ginsberg and Orlovksy were touring Britain at the time and our house was a natural stopping point – they had introduced my father to America and now it was our turn to introduce them to Gloucestershire. They got the best introduction possible to the wilds of the valley; the car that they had arrived in was not inclined to take kindly to treacherous conditions and the weather had turned, bringing sheets of rain and fallen leaves up the valleys from the Severn. The concrete road and its craftily steep hairpin bend were as slippery as a skating rink and, as we attempted to set off for Stroud, the car stuck fast on the hairpin, teetering on the edge of the tree line and threatening to descend into our house.

The Beat Generation's arrival into Stroud was momentarily off the road, so all hands leapt out of the car, and leaned in to haul the machine back into action. It was always a hill for scaring people. The poet Harry Fainlight, a fey, gentle and eccentric poet who had read with my father and Ginsberg at the International Poetry Incarnation at the Albert Hall in 1965 and who was notorious for willing cars to stop if he did not want to go anywhere, effected a breakdown of our car on the same hill. Harry would come to visit us every so often in the early 1970s. My memories of him are distant, but entirely at odds with the sometimes violent extremes of his poetry. I recall a very soulful, gentle presence who would listen to me attentively, however slight and fantastical my verbal wanderings, and would adventure with me in words. The car started again with a growl and a gronk only after my mother had turned in her seat, looked Harry in the eye as he sat in the back of the car next to me, and told him, with delicate, tender command, that it had been lovely to see him but it was time to be moving on.

That hill also nearly took my life, aged six. My mother was going away to give a reading and I was to stay with the Lloyds. We drove up the hill in the new silver Renault, just past the bend and she parked outside the steps up to the Lloyds' front door, putting the handbrake on as she handed my bag of things to Jean. I was procrastinating in the passenger seat.

'Come on out of there, Adam,' my mother called.

'Come on Adam,' yelled Katy, eager to take command, to play.

'All right! I'm coming,' I replied, stepping over to the driver's seat and losing my balance as I negotiated my way past the steering wheel. I reached out and grabbed the first thing I could find to steady myself – the handbrake, set in the front and middle of the old-style Renault, to the left of the dashboard and down.

The handbrake moved, and so did the car; it slipped gently backwards down the hill, gathering pace. I threw myself to the floor, watching trees spin past above me, hearing nothing but roaring in my ears, clutching hard to the base of the passenger seat. My mother, my father, Jean and Katy stood above the steps down to the road, transfixed, I am told, quite unable to move or speak as the car disappeared into the woods, down the dirt track that had once been the main road to Slad. The car span and, fortunately for me, wedged between two trees – I was a hair's breadth away from rolling down the hill.

Only then did anyone move. Katy screamed, I think. My mother came billowing down the hill, composure forgotten. She pulled me from the well of the car and hugged me tighter than I could bear, her breath heavy against my shaking chest, my hair wet with her tears.

I suspect the Lloyds were watching on again as Ginsberg, Orlovsky, Pickard and my father heaved in the wet to get the car started in 1979. A show was always there to be had when my father was involved, and I have good reason to know that they enjoyed many of them. Eventually, after much shouting, grunting and amused, verse-fuelled invective, the car was once again as roadworthy as it was ever likely to be and we were off.

Even now, decades later, I meet people who came to that reading behind Starters café, who tell me that they remember me reading poems with Allen Ginsberg and my parents on Bonfire Night, aged eight, a little orange-headed blur of composed enthusiasm. Looking back through the papers I have kept, I find continual evidence of my parents' hand in encouraging me to write. The 'Plastic Farmyard Poem' my father cobbled together out of things I said aged three ('I see a rainbow/in the radio/in the music/in the bed/– I hear ladies/ singing/in my head'), which he then presented to me as a poem that I had written and he had edited. There was a poem about autumn, which I wrote alone and entered into a school competition. It didn't win anything because, as one of the teachers told my mother, they suspected other pens than mine had had a hand in it. My eight-year-old redhead's temper was incandescent over the injustice of that.

I learned from both my parents to listen to the rhythm of words. I learned an ear for poetry that most schools hammer out of one by insisting on ascribing meaning and discussing intent at a forge when such things should be rolled out slowly in calm pastures, over time. My father taught me to play with words, to bounce them ebulliently around the tongue, to find rhythm, to find the sense in nonsense and the nonsense in sense. My mother taught me about breath and silence, about stillness and how to pick music from a murmuring core of silence, about the colour of words, about looking and hearing and thinking and dreaming.

The poems I read with Ginsberg on Guy Fawkes Night, aged eight, were not very good – charming enough for a child, as pure as any child's writing can be if they're given the chance to be free – but the lessons that came with them stayed with me, as did the sounds of the valley. These have driven nearly everything I've written as an adult, much of which stems from a long conversation with my mother's writing and with the places that were important to us; the only real communication I was able to go on having with her, since she died when I was twelve. Death and absence taught me how to begin to write.

6

You'll Be Kissed Again

The valley was undergoing a multilateral evacuation in 1980. As low-flying jets from Fairford whizzed overhead, the free-thinking party of the 1970s crawled to an end as all the families that had come there began to move away and a procession of holidaymakers and weekenders moved on in.

The Hortons moved to Australia, leaving a blank at the end of the garden. The land had been open for years; our gardens were as one and the children ran between them endlessly, through rows of potatoes my father had grown after a potato blight and a rhubarb patch that remained persistent until new neighbours built a wall right through it and stopped the rhubarb dead.

I was immediately sad about that blank space – no more parties filled with small girls who found me endlessly fascinating and were prepared to show it. I wasn't sure what to make of the attention, but I knew I'd miss it. I had come home along the garden one afternoon wet-faced and bewildered after visiting the Hortons. I think I must have been eight.

'What's the matter?' my mother asked.

I didn't know quite what to say.

'Nobody hurt you did they?' she asked, crouching and cupping my face in her hand.

'No,' I said. 'A girl wouldn't stop kissing me.'

'Wouldn't stop?' she said.

'No.'

'Did you ask her to stop?'

'No,' I said, a little mulish. I think she may have laughed.

'Didn't you like being kissed?'

'No. Yes. I don't know,' I said. I can still remember the girl's warm mouth pressed on mine as she sat on my lap, telling me I was funny and hugging my neck as I sat there contemplating the strangeness of it all. She was six, I think, and charmed by my white skin and my red hair. She liked my freckles too. She kept on kissing me and calling to others in the garden and talking, as if it was the most natural thing in the world to do. Then a jet flew over, scratching its belly on the treetops and roaring like a wounded dragon. We flung ourselves to the floor and the kissing stopped, became crying. I remember Judy Horton flat on the floor and cursing, words I had only heard before from my mother in a towering rage. I ran home, wet-faced, frightened, not sure if it was the kissing or the plane that scared me most.

'You'll be kissed again,' my mother said. 'It's not so strange.'

Some people, at least, were moving in to stay. Pat and Hans Hopf, whose sons John and Robert had been fast friends with Jules and Jamie Lloyd when they came at weekends, moved down to the valley permanently in 1979 in a cloud of sweet-smelling pipe smoke, taking up residence at the other end of our little terrace in a house they'd owned since 1963. I instantly, cheekily renamed them Hat and Pans, much to my father's delight.

Hans was a stocky German, his pipe in constant motion between hand and mouth, a gruffly cheerful man whom I associate mostly with clouds of tobacco and pesticide, standing in his immaculate garden raising a hand in greeting and warning me off cycling too fast down the path past his front door, having seen me crash my first bike spectacularly outside it the first time I rode it, taking the skin from my knees. Pat was (and remains) quietly indomitable and kind.

Hans came prepared for the worst, with snow chains for his car, having seen winter's obliteration howl through the valley many times, long before I was born. Sometimes, walking past their house now, I still smell the sweet tobacco smoke and hear him calling out his perennial, thickly accented cry of 'Do not play ball on my land!'

What was strangest to me was that Katy was leaving too, Katy whose valley this was as much as mine, my sister in all but blood, who even now can see through me to the truth and call it without resentment (or too much, anyway) on my part. Katy, who when I got a stuffed fox in a dandyish red waistcoat for Christmas, had had to have a stuffed fox herself to avoid resentment and arguments and jealousies. Katy, who my cousin Zoë (two years older than myself) had accused of being 'a bit too big for her boots' as we walked down the steep slope, away from St Benedicts; Katy had tried to lead the way in every game and Zoë, also used to getting her own way, had led an uncomfortable revolt as I sat rigid on the fence. Katy, who had suffered my illnesses when I succumbed to them because her parents had sent her down to see me, making sure she got them out of the way. In bed with mumps and tonsillitis, I remember the frown haloed by her mop of unruly white blonde hair, her concern. A few weeks later, better, I remember her grumbling fury at me as I sat by her bed, eating the grapes I'd brought as consolation for the mumps she'd taken home.

Before the Lloyds left, midway through 1980, a few months before my mother and I, they moved into the dark old haunted house at the end of the valley. The snows had come and Katy was ill and bored. I packed up my collections of *Beano* and *Dandy* comics, dragged them down on the sledge for her to read. Taking them home a week later in the thaw, slush, shivering down from the naked rafters of the abbey of trees, destroyed every single one. I remember weeping with fury as Desperate Dan was mulched to pulp, the ink merging

Jocks with Geordies whilst Chips melted into Bully Beef and Korky shrank away to nothing.

So much was changing, merging, having the colour washed from it. The valley was emptying itself, melting away, taking childhood with it.

Mullions, by Jane Percival, 1974.

Cows on Swift's Hill.

Left: An abbey of trees. Above: Cloudscapes over Slad.

Adam, Katy Lloyd and Jessie Horton, by Alan Lloyd.

Cows at the Roman bridge.

The front room at Mullions, by Diana Lodge.

Piedmont, a thumb offshoot of the Slad Valley.

Through the trees to Slad.

The path to Slad.

Overlooking Slad.

Mullions now.

Trees in Piedmont growing over the stones.

Catswood.

Sheep at the top of Steanbridge Lane.

The quarry at Swift's Hill.

End of the road, Steanbridge Lane.

Looking to Stroud from Swift's Hill.

Swift's Hill from the Vatch.

Frances Horovitz in the Slad Valley, by Oswald Jones.

Diana Lodge, by Jessie Ann Matthew.

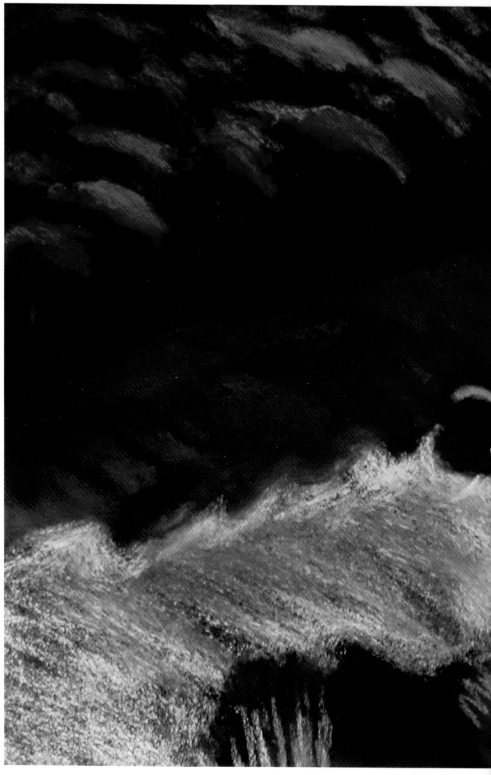

Low Light in November from Swift's Hill, by Carolyn White, from the collection of Rob and Jehanne

Mehta, photographed by Fred Chance.

Overlooking Steanbridge Lane.

Rose Cottage in Elcombe.

Slad from Swift's Hill.

Old gates at the Vatch–Elcombe junction.

The approach to Slad up Steanbridge Lane.

At the sign of the Woolpack.

Slad church.

Slad.

The Woolpack by night.

Slad by lamplight.

A pint or three at the Woolpack.

Inside the Woolpack, Laurie Lee keeping a watchful eye on the instruments.

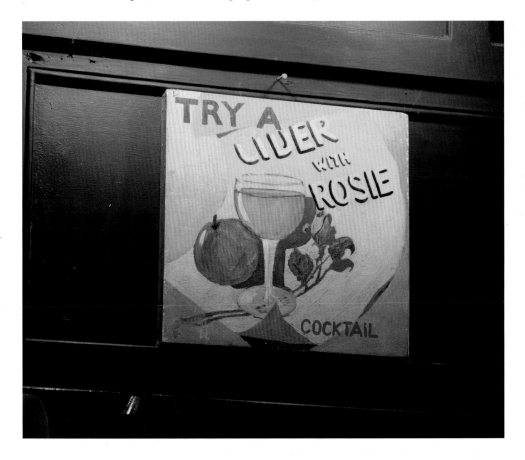

Swift's Hill framed by the Woolpack's back window.

A misty day looking towards Stroud from the hill above Steanbridge Lane.

Adam and Katy Lloyd, by Alan Lloyd.

The lake in which a woman drowned in *Cider with Rosie* and in which the author of this book discovered many leeches.

Overlooking the Slad racing stables.

The Roman bridge near Snows Farm, overgrown.

A 'polite' bridge replacing an old ford.

The rotting shed at Mullions.

Mullions. Pulled from the shed and abandoned in cut-down yew branches. 'Somebody must have an orphanage for/All those things that nobody wants any more.' (Tom Waits, 'Broken Bicycles')

Midsummer Morning Log Jam

I n 1984, a year after my mother died, I came back to the Slad Valley in a blank state, against my mother's dying wishes, much of my memory of childhood scrubbed away by grief. I came back to live with my father, who for four years I had seen only in school holidays and more often than not in London, dancing through a street party with him for the 1981 royal wedding or pestering him into taking me to an all-day showing of the Star Wars trilogy.

The only time I remember visiting him in the valley with my mother in those years away, living in Sunderland and Herefordshire, was when she drove me through Slad to the last clot of tarmac before the road ran out at Snows Farm, having called my father from the phone box next to the Woolpack to let him know we were near. Setting out again, she narrowly avoided hitting two boys playing football on Steanbridge Lane, at the top of the hill before the steep descent down to the drowning pool. I remember her cursing herself and at their carelessness, shaking as she drove on down the hill and fretting as we awaited my father by the house at the end of the road.

He arrived in a huff of lateness, upset that she had come that way instead of down the perilous road from Bisley and that she would not come into the house. For my sake, the argument was muted,

In Painswick Churchyard
Is this where people are buried?
I will not let them bury you

He picnics among tombs
pours imaginary tea,
a yew tree his kitchen

You will live with me in my house

Oh could I believe the living and dead
inhabit one house under the sky

and you my child run into your future
for ever
Frances Horovitz

saved for letters or past-my-bedtime phone calls – the last huge row
of their separation I had witnessed was in the summer of 1980, over
books. Aged nine, and long protected from such vicious and point-
less disputes, I had withdrawn into the corner by the door, under a
poster that stated 'Anyone caught smoking on these premises will
be hung by the toenails and pummelled into unconsciousness with
an organic carrot'; a tourist token, decorated with cartoon Native
Americana, from my father's tours of California reading poetry to
beatified literature students in Berkeley, UCLA, Stamford et al.

'Stop it,' I yelled at them as they sniped and squealed about
which book belonged to whom. 'You're behaving like stupid, small
CHILDREN!'

There had been arguments before, of course, and my mother
could be fierce and satirical when the need arose, with either my
father or myself. Her closest friend, Jane Percival, came to stay
one night, out of the blue and through the rain, despairing of the
strained relationship with her husband at their home in Somerset.
She had driven up in the dark, in urgent need of the comforting
shoulder of her friend. My mother tenderly invited her in and, sitting her by the wood-burning stove, fed her homemade cakes and
tea. I was lying on the couch, off school for a couple of days with
a slight cold. I waved to Jane, who started to speak and, as she did
so, shakily lit a cigarette. My father came down the stairs, an ex-
smoker of evangelical proportions, who had quit his twelve-year
addictions to Players Mild, along with whatever forms of mari-
juana came his way, soon after we moved into the cottage, and
never looked back.

I coughed a little as he opened the door. He turned to Jane and
demanded she put the cigarette out.

'Can't you see you're making him cough?' he said, waving in my
direction dramatically before sitting by me and cuddling my shoulders.

'I'm alright,' I said, trying to sit up, unheard as the row escalated
and Jane was banished over the garden to stay with the Hortons,
where, thanks to the regular incursions of strangely scented
Saturday night smoke drifting over to our house almost as effectively as their renditions of Dylan, my mother knew she would be
made welcome, smoker or not. My mother went with her, to make

the arrangements, almost smoking herself as she reached the tipsy-toploftical pinnacle of a towering rage.

I was hurried into bed, huddled up the stairs in my father's arms, and listened enthralled and terrified as my mother's fury vented itself downstairs when she came home. It was carefully modulated, her anger, as was everything she did, as precise and quietly explosive as her movements. (This was a woman who would buy a Mars bar, divide it into five slivers and keep them in the fridge, eating one piece a day at most over the course of a week – and who would pick daintily at the immaculately prepared and considered food she cooked as if it were a meal in a play or a film, which you were only supposed to pretend to eat).

My father matched her with his more expansive, discursive and diversionary modes, running little rivulets of counter-argument in the defence of my health past her, trying to wear down the barricades of the Stanislavskian fourth wall she had built around her outrage. She simmered like an Ibsen heroine. He danced his tongue around the argument like an angry Puck.

Living in the valley again after four years away was a strange experience, without my mother or any families or children my age there to temper it and tame it. The valley had existed in me as a state of perfection, a place where everything was right with the world, which blurred with the roseate tinge of half-forgotten allegiances and love. It was far less rewarding to explore alone, back in the reality of it – the dry stone walls seemed less sure of themselves, more careworn and mossy with inattention, the homes-from-home that Katy and I had built in tangled copses were small and run down, empty of the fantastically mundane lives that she and I had created in them for ourselves.

The valley was a place of importance to my father, too. A giddy nostalgia possessed us both, for the time we'd spent with chickens and the attempted smallholding dreams of food for free, basking in my mother's presence from 1971 to 1979, all interruptions and absences forgotten or set aside.

He remembered me as that child, however, happy and piping down the valleys wild, unburdened by any sorrow greater than the shock of finding a large dead rabbit in the kitchen (brought in proudly by Arwen, her best Queen of Sheba purr rattling in her throat) not long after I'd finished reading *Watership Down* and was still lost in the heady afterglow of rabbit sympathy. I had come back a teenager, mourning the loss of that happiness, the loss of my mother, hormones rasping slowly into gear under the buzzing throttle-roar of grief like a low-flying jet. Inevitably, as it would with any father and son left to their own devices even under the easiest of circumstances, it led to conflict; on-running disagreements that coloured the times when all was otherwise well. Memories, pleasant and otherwise, spilled over into the present too often, exposed it to unflattering scrutiny. We warred over the fact that I was growing up.

Whilst I had been in Sunderland, living with my mother and Roger, my father had engaged with the valley as best he could, unable to be there all that often, what with earning a living in London and the personal disconnectedness of the cottage. The happiness he had so enjoyed living there with my mother and I meant that return-ing there, apart from the expense of travel and upkeep, was another source of sorrowing at our having left. During one of his longer absences during the heavy winter of 1981, the pipes had burst because he had forgotten to switch off the water on his previous sojourn, and when the thaw came, the water attempted to reclaim the house. Arwen, who was too much a cat of the valley to be torn away to Sunderland with us, survived as best she could, becom-ing a little more feral – when my father was away, she was fed by the Hopfs. My father felt the perhaps inevitably depressing void of both my and my mother's absence from the cottage and the valley intensely. Both of us had become so deeply entwined there that reflections of the decade-long occupations of our bodies and spirits were always palpable.

He had come back most often in the spring, in the height of summer and in the early gold of autumn, the valley being an unre-lenting place to live in alone in winter, and would spend time in the valley writing and jogging down the lane to Driftcombe by way of exercise. He often jogged off wearing the dark green eyeshade that deepened the greens of the abbey of trees and which he was rarely un-shaded by when the sun came cantering over the hill when I was young. That eyeshade pursues my memories of him throughout the valley everywhere they go, and occasionally it pursues me out of the valley. As a child it was a source of fascination and embarrassment, an item of clothing that made him stand out and be noticed. Sometimes I would try wearing it, sat on a high-backed chair in his attic pretending to type, only for the elastic to slip around my neck making the eyeshade fall to my chest like a bib.

I rarely tried it on after he went swimming in Stroud pool with Katy Lloyd and me. My father entered the pool shortly after Katy and I had leapt in and had started splashing about. There was a sudden ripple of laughter; we looked around and there at the edge of the pool stood my father, in a shower cap bunched up like a squid on his head and held in place by his eyeshade, his heavy spectacles perched on his nose and sporting a pair of voluminous and (happily) far from revealing underpants in place of trunks. People had noticed and were laughing and pointing. Katy and I, appalled, swam as far in the other direction as we could manage, wishing ourselves invisible. It was no use; he submerged himself in the pool, calling joyfully to us, and came swimming in our direction, the eyeshade jutting out of the water like a lopsided shark's fin. We fled, cannoning around the pool until at last, exhausted, it was time to escape into the changing rooms. I cannot, even now, swim in Stroud pool without the hot flush of childish shame clutching at my throat.

Taking exercise with my father was often embarrassing. He would wave me goodbye from the bottom of the lane by doing would-be star jumps, and singing loudly whenever I left in a car as I waved from the rear window – fascinated or horrified depending upon who was in the car with me. As a teenager I would clam up, ashamed of his gusto, and rapidly stop playing if anyone walked past whilst we were engaged in the eccentric game of 'hand tennis' we invented. This was a cross between tennis and volleyball, which involved our batting a huge yellow foam ball across the privet hedges and dry stone walls we claimed as nets. Yet the exercise he took alone in the valley, in the long emptiness when my mother and I were gone, was far from embarrassing. Without us there he noticed the things we had noticed together in a greater detail than he had before, collecting them in his head as he jogged up and down the valley and piecing together a 670-line poem of such rural intensity as might dispel Robert Graves' assertion that he was 'incorrigibly urban', a *Midsummer Morning Jog Log*:

> ... apparition I must seem, leaping blind and deaf
> to the fleet-winged early warning
> notes of my advent
> relayed from the lanesides
> all over the valley

> – so brutishly revelling
> in my refracted halo, vicarious godhead
> of being

> – The First up
> and out – ha!
> jigging and bopping
> with ludicrously heavy-booted feet
> to avoid the upsurge here
> of a sun-spatted puddle,
> there the liquidation
> of an innocent slug or snail ...

Coming back to live with him as *Midsummer Morning Jog Log* was being finished, I relished his renewed and vigorous interest in the valley. I followed him on jogs down to Driftcombe, followed in turn by Arwen at a discreet distance, both of us a little too wary to galumph as vigorously as him. I took photos for him, some of which were sent to the book's illustrator, Peter Blake, deep in his rural-ist phase – the five-barred gate in the book is drawn from a picture I took. Yet although my father and I romped and roamed together through the valley's summer effulgence for a while, running and dreaming and laughing, the creeping grief that had been building in me finally struck home.

My father was the youngest of ten refugee children brought over from Germany in 1937, escaping the Nazis at the last minute, thanks in part to my Grandfather's connections with the banking family Rothschild, for whom he was working as a lawyer. Raised almost as much by his four sisters and nanny as by his mother, he was ill conditioned to cope with day-to-day necessities such as cooking. Many of the meals we ate together in the house were prepared by me from the small stock of recipes my mother had taught me when we were living on Hadrian's Wall with Roger in the winters of 1981 and 1982.

This only changed when Inge came to visit, a stylish and beautiful woman my father had met two years after my mother and I left for Sunderland. She was German, and Jewish, and had come to London in the 1960s only a few years after she had discovered that she had survived the war not knowing that her mother was Jewish, nor anything of the constant danger she was in as a child in Nazi Germany.

She worked for Lufthansa and as a translator for Vidal Sassoon, and was a gentle, harmonious presence in the house whenever she came to stay, and not just because I was relieved of cooking duty when she was there (though a sticker I made and stuck to the wall above the archaic stove stating that 'Inge is a fab cook' was an indication of how relieved I really was). She also taught me how to iron and made me dance with her to Ken Colyer's New Orleans jazz around the front room, trying hard as I could to imitate her sprightly, delicate hops; she did all she could to be a motherly influence on my life.

She, too, attempted to stem the tide of papers that flowed through my father's attic room, but they spread unstoppably regardless, leaking down through the floorboards into the kitchen, where an erratic and rusty old filing cabinet now occupied one corner of the room, making it harder to seat guests round the kitchen table. The stair-cupboard, which had once been an airy little space, its shelves filled with tools for the garden, useful bits of string, scissors, a sewing kit, Wellingtons, fuses, light bulbs and boxes of emergency candles left over from the three-day week, now groaned with paperwork crushed in to leave room for just a few rusting and wood-wormed garden tools.

The garden was fast becoming jungle, barring us in with 'barricades of weeds revolutionary–/weeds upon weeds in abundancy swirling/and thrusting their spears in brazen pride ...'[1] We fought back with rusty scythes and bill-hooks, and with the inadequate strimmer that trembled like a cornered rabbit whenever we introduced it to brambles or to the relentless nettles that shot up everywhere and were too far gone for soup. Tears filled our eyes for the neat rows of vegetables long gone, whose 'seedpacket pennanted rows' flickered in the mind's eye like some great medieval pageant ground shrunk down by time, rubbed away by the slow, shadow-hungry creep of the trees.

It was home, and it felt almost as though my mother was there, whispering in the trees when the wind picked up, or sending a wren waltzing in through my bedroom window when I was thinking of her: it settled for a moment on the side of my desk, cocked its head, lifted its tail and flew out again, a flash of powdery brown as its wings spread out, like a sharply angled cartoon version of her favourite floppy hat. But without allies to fall back on living near at hand, and without a car to escape in, the house was too close a cage for us both. We rubbed each other raw.

---

1 From *Midsummer Morning Jog Log*.

8

Changing the Record

Grief is rarely a permanent fog of affliction, rolling up the valleys of the brain and refusing to leave, and I had the sudden yellow flare of winter jasmine up the cold cottage wall on an otherwise bleak late winter morning to help salve the mists of sorrow and self-pity that coursed through me; the usual teenage hormonal aggravations simmering alongside the loss of my mother and the fact that none of my friends lived nearer than four miles away.

The sun ran in yolky rivulets through the horizon at sunset. In summer rain I sat out under the yew boughs, watching the rain shift like a modest bride up to the valley's head, the spring's ravenous mouth. I cycled to school often, since a 6 a.m. wake-up call to catch the 8.30 a.m. bus was rarely easy to achieve, spent too long marvelling at the rhythms of ploughing, going slow to argue with sheep in the orchard on the side of the road before Sydenhams Farm or peering over the wall into the old pig sty. At two I would call out 'Big pig kippit' to them as they slept – as my father insisted on telling visitors, including the attractive young women who came to do occasional secretarial work for him and whose attentions, in some cases, I would have far rather had been focused on what I considered to be my more adult charms.

School was a relief, once I had extracted myself from the local boys' grammar school, too brutish and testosterone-fuelled a place for a thirteen-year-old still grieving the loss of his mother. Instead, I went to Archway, the mixed comprehensive with a radical staff, the school where my mother had taught eight years before. I was welcomed in by teachers who had known her well, but none of whom made that fact explicit for at least a couple of years, which helped the process of settling in no end.

More important, there were friends to be made, new confidantes as well as old allies. Skanda Huggins was there, a year below me in school years but the first person I called and told when I was accepted there. New friends were made – Mackie, Giz, Legzee, Joe, Matthew Chadwick and Mathew Shaw (with both of whom I'd hunted for Easter eggs at Diana Lodge's house years before), plus Euan and many more. We bonded mostly over music, and my ability to concentrate slipped a gear thanks to late-night sessions of listening to John Peel on BBC Radio 1.

Music became as essential to me as breathing at about fourteen, as it has for huge numbers of British teenagers born post-Second World War. I ripped up the cottage with anything from Prince to Charlie Mingus, the Dead Kennedys to The The, raiding Woolworths and the Trading Post in Stroud with my pocket money after school, or ransacking my father's record collection for something – anything – new, straining through the lyrics for inspiration and points of identification and jumping to the rhythms that Slad and the valley could not or would not provide.

My father, when lost in his attic with work, would hammer away at his typewriter in competition with the chattering bird we never accurately identified (although we suspected it might be a blackbird) and which we dubbed the typewriter bird as it seemed to want to talk back to his erratically speedy, one-finger typing from the nearest treetop. Often he would yell down the stairs for some peace, for the space to think clearly as I span records on the tired old blue and white Dansette, which allowed me to play singles at 16 or 78rpm, much to my amusement and my father's regular annoyance.

Eventually the Dansette wore out and even my father, who was happy enough for me to be playing Mingus every so often, even if

he noisily pretended to object to Prince or the post-punk and electronica I began to discover going cheap at car boot sales, decided we
should get a new record player. The trouble was, as ever, that money
was tight, so we looked in the local paper for weeks, eventually finding a cheap but cheerful looking player someone was advertising.
We phoned and asked if we could come and try it. The sellers said
yes, of course.

The next difficulty was how to get there. My father had never
learned to drive; his only two attempts had nearly ended in disaster:
first in Ireland when he had myopically come close to running the
car into a couple of cows on a road trip visiting poets and second
when my mother, in despair of being the only driver in the house
had, in the early 1970s, tried to get him to drive out of the valley, up
the steep hill that ran behind our house and round the hairpin bend
that has terrified even the calmest of drivers who have come at it
unwary over the years. That time, the car nearly tipped over the edge
and back down the hill onto our house. My mother commanded
him to never drive again.

This didn't make it easy to live in the valley – getting to school in
Stroud was a mission that involved waking at 6 a.m., with or before
the dawn as a farm worker would have, and cycling two miles to the
bus, which as I got older I invariably missed. Even getting post out
was a trial and given that my father was sending out magazines on
mail order, and could rarely spare the time away from his typewriter
to walk over-burdened with post to the nearest tiny letterbox, neighbours had to be asked. A small community will willingly give help
when help is needed, but favours need to be spread out. I remember
my father checking the back of Alan Lloyd's Land Rover for the letters
he'd asked Alan to post, and which Alan often forgot, sometimes quite
deliberately. Getting shopping back was an equally arduous task.

The Lloyds were long gone, however, and there were new resi-
dents in their long, strangely Alpine cottage. Hugh Padgham, with
whom I was impressed because he talked music with me occasionally as if my tastes mattered, had moved in not long after I came
back to the valley. I remember him at one of our first encounters
being cheerfully derisive of the Madonna badge I was wearing. On
looking closer, he told me that I at least had *some* good taste. I was

also wearing a Sting badge, entirely unaware that Hugh had just produced the album the badge was promoting, and that he had produced The Police.

My father, wondering how to get to the house wherein the record player was waiting, had an epiphany. He picked up the phone.

'Hi Hugh,' he said. 'May I ask a favour?'

A moment's silence, then: 'Well, we've found a second hand record player for sale and I was hoping we might be able to get a lift to test it out. Since you're here this weekend, I hoped you might be able to take us, as you know quite a bit about record players.'

The conversation went on a little while, my father's charm offensive picking up apace, until finally Hugh closed the dialogue with the suggestion that we find a record with which to test the player when we got there.

Hugh greeted us with what seems to me now to be a gently arch, friendly amusement at the top of the hill some hours later, and drove us off to see the record player. It wasn't the most comfortable of rides for me. I was all too easily embarrassed by my father's persuasions and felt discomfited by the idea that the producer of The Police was being dragged along to help us buy a cheap record player because he 'knew about this sort of thing'.

Hugh, to be fair, seemed to let the whole thing breeze past him until we got to the house, where my father introduced him to the record player's owner with all due pomp and I withered a little more. The owner got the record player started and I put on the record I had chosen to bring. It was *Unknown Pleasure,* by Joy Division, which I had found at a car boot sale the week before and was desperate to play.

'What do you think?' my father asked Hugh, referring to the record player.

'It's all right, if you like that sort of thing,' said Hugh, referring to the album, which was just the sort of dark and monumentally, majestically tortured music favoured by a sixteen-year-old of melancholic disposition. Madonna and Sting were long gone from my affections by this time.

I said nothing, withering still more. The album sounded fine, if a little thin on the cheap, tinny but fairly functional record player. We bought the machine. My music collection lived to shout down bird-song and my father's attempts to work another day. I don't recall that we ever asked a similar favour of Hugh again.

It was hard to get excited by music four miles out of the teen-age social whirl of a small town, where there's too often little else to do but listen to music in company and get mutually excited about it. I wasn't particularly musical, and could not have busked round Spain as Laurie Lee had, having learned the violin as a child. Although Inge loaned me a trumpet and tried to help me learn it, I gave up because it was too awkward to take to school on the back of my bicycle. A trumpet needed accompaniment, the added textures of people and instruments, to get me excited by its sound. Laurie, with a violin, could make music purely for himself, or with others, as he pleased.

The big bands had also long since stopped coming to Stroud. The Beatles' worst gig was in Stroud's Subscription Rooms in the month they made it big, Paul McCartney has gone on record as saying (although several people's favourite aunties were apparently walked home by Macca that night). U2 are notoriously supposed to have played to the proverbial three men and an asthmatic dog in the Marshall Rooms just before they became huge.

So it was fortunate that my father needed to go to London regu-larly for work and arranged for me to stay with friends dotted around the five valleys of Stroud; with the Mackintoshes, the Huggins family and with the Lloyds, who soon moved to the other end of the Slad Valley, into a bungalow that Alan began to do up, as he had done with many properties since they left the house above me in the valley in 1980. I found music any way I could.

I had come back to the valley with a handful of memories and poems – by my parents, by Laurie Lee, Dylan Thomas and Charles Causley – locked in my head as the only reminders of childhood, ripe as just plucked plums on my tongue. With a gang of friends and places to stay, the valley's people finally began to come to life around me again, a wider spectrum of people and influences to show me how much the place had changed. And then, suddenly, Laurie was there again, marking the way.

9

Are You Writing?

Laurie seemed to appear over the horizon with surprising regularity after my return. First, we held a party in 1985 to celebrate birthdays and returns, and a party in the valley wasn't quite a party without Laurie. The garden, rougher now than it had been when my mother was alive, and no longer given over to vegetables since my father was going too regularly to London for work to risk the expense of growing food and forgetting to water it and tend its stems against the constant hordes of slug and rabbit, badger and the occasional, tentative, greedy deer, became a rolling picnic table we had laid out in a panic, spreading our erratic party wares across the strimmed and hewn-down expanses of woodland undergrowth.

Old friends were there in abundance; Diana Lodge stomped over the valley from Trillgate, the Lloyds came back down to the valley for the day, Jane Percival came with her daughters, and if she smoked while she was there it was far down the garden and out of scent, away from my father's disapproving glare.

Laurie's arrival, with his wife Kathy, garrulous and dressed in white, caused the usual stir. Laurie announced his presence in our front room with a cheerful abandonment, filling the room with a personality as wide and welcoming and mischievous as his

outstretched arms. I was on hand with a camera and caught him as he stretched out in greeting, his flies undone and a huge smile on his face.

'Are you writing?' he asked me later, once someone had pointed out his exposed underpants with a friendly laugh and the offer of a drink. He was perched on a stool, and I felt a little overawed.

'A little,' I said. 'I'm going to a summer class with Gillian Clarke in a few weeks.'

I pointed Gillian out, my mother's close friend who had on instinct travelled up to London the day before she'd died to see her, thinking it might be the last chance she had. She had come down from Wales for the day to celebrate with us and also to make sure I was settling in acceptably with my father.

'Ah, writing classes,' said Laurie, and he raised his eyebrows and smiled. 'Do you need them when you've got all this?'

He gestured to the party, the valley, the world at large, his drink slopping a little, like late winter sunlight over the edge of his glass.

I wanted to say that it was the class my mother had taught before she died, that it kept me focused, that it was a connection to her. Before any words could leave my lips, Laurie pressed his hand to my shoulder, smiled again and was gone for a refresher, to talk to others. I slipped back into the party and to other friends, looking to the valley with new eyes.

I dug out Laurie's poems again after this, exploring the recent edition of his *Selected Poems* I had found on my father's shelves, looking for further clues to his meaning. In 'The Abandoned Shade' I found these lines:

Season and landscape's liturgy,
badger and sneeze of rain,
the bleat of bats, the bounce of rabbits
bubbling under the hill:

Each old and echo-salted tongue
sings to my backward glance;
but the voice of the boy, the boy I seek,
within my mouth is dumb.

So I made the valley my study, at the expense of school, even so far as to take my war with mathematics to a ritualistic extreme, carrying my hated maths homework book out into the woods and burning it with hysterical ceremony on a pyre, shouting a curse on all algebra into the slow dusk as moths came battering their way towards the flames. I sought out the voice of the boy I had been, a process that continues as surely as the stream runs under the bridge, as seasons shift and find new ways to express themselves.

It paid off, this study of landscape, became, three years later, the first poem I wrote that marked for me the change up from the pretty poems of childish preoccupation and the bleak angst of teenage fear (although it combines elements of each). It was written on one of Gillian's courses, but it looked back at the Slad Valley with a keener eye than I had managed before.

An Owl Breaks the Silence

In the deepening contrast
between night and day

when an owl breaks the silence
and the foxes bay

when the chattering chaffinch
lays down its tune

and tissue moths
flit past the moon

when millions of fireflies
wisp in the dusk

and the butterfly's cocoon
is merely a husk

when the badger is starting
its nightly round

and the rabbit is keeping
its nose to the ground

when snails creep out
from under rocks

and the chicken begins
to forget the fox

then the humans in offices
will do something rash

and when it snows
will it snow ice or ash?

Encounters with Laurie were relatively rare before I was old enough to drink in a pub; the Woolpack was too much a local's place to get away with brazening a pint aged sixteen or seventeen – I had The Pelican in Stroud for that, part vice-den for the traveller community, part working man's sinkhole, a pub that promised anarchy and table football and the chance to stare forlornly as the girls from school one fancied were being picked off one by one by older men. Or there were small off-licences selling Thunderbird, a toxic, chemical-addled perry which stripped brain cells, stomach lining and, if you were really lucky, inhibitions. No first long drink of golden fire, this. Never to be forgotten, perhaps, this acrid precursor of alcopops, which stung like factory smoke and clouded the eyes to reason. It made even the occasional quarter bottle of bad blended whisky taste like nectar. Never to be forgotten. Never, please god, to be tasted again.

Once I reached pub age, however, I saw him every so often in the Woolpack, exchanging pleasantries with him and occasionally talking a little about poetry before moving on. Some of the most memorable encounters with him, however, tended to take place in the impersonal surroundings of Stroud railway station.

Coming back from college, hauling a heavy backpack, I encountered Laurie several times at the beginning of his canter home from London and the Chelsea Arts Club literary high life through the pubs of Stroud: one at the Imperial, one at the Shunters and see where else might be reached before hitting the Woolpack and home, a rascally glint in his eye and Kathy next to him, making sure that nothing went wrong.

Charming and just a little bit roguish, Laurie was always a pleasure to meet when gently in his cups; in these high and expansive times he was a purveyor of the finest, most convincing-sounding whoppers and shaggy dog stories to admiring passers-by, glancing over his glasses to see how much was being swallowed. He told people in all seriousness that the planning department was intending to raze Slad and build a motorway through the valley, much to the delight of those he pranked, and he constantly suggested to people that it would be inadvisable for them to get him to sign their copy of *Cider with Rosie* as it was the 'rare, unsigned copies that made money nowadays'.

Laurie was also known to take his new wireless landline phone to the pub with him, his house being near enough down the hill to pick up a signal, and he would apparently hush his drinking buddies when calls came, in a most likely vain effort to conceal his whereabouts. He didn't keep this impish attitude just for the pub, however; when a newspaper called his friend Val Hennessey to ask her to update his obituary, Laurie, who happened to be there when the call came, took enormous delight in trying to persuade her to let him write it with her and fabricate it utterly.

Beneath this easy charm lay what seemed to me to be a seam of sadness, however. 'It isn't easy to write in the country,' he told the *New York Times* in 1993, after *A Moment of War* came out. 'Either it's a nice day and you lie in the long grass, or people knock on your door and want you to go to the pub for a chat. And that's that day gone.'

It can't be easy to follow up a success as widespread and all consuming as *Cider with Rosie*, either. I remember the Stroud launch of *A Moment of War*, in the echoing concrete cavern of the town's starkly municipal leisure centre. The worthies and celebrants gathered in the high mezzanine corridor overlooking the game courts, their words confused and amplified by the architecture, Babel-bound in the baffling surroundings. There were a great many people there, but the building contrived to make it feel as though there were only ever ten or so people milling around and sipping wine, whilst Laurie sat with signing pen in hand at a table piled high with books looking a little forlorn, though he cheered up considerably when familiar faces came to chat.

Whatever the reasons for the slow-down in his writing life, it didn't stop him from appreciating and pushing others, and this is where my meetings with him became a joy.

'Ah, Adam,' he'd cry, Kathy smiling warmly at his side. 'Are you writing?'

I'd make my best excuses, saying I was keeping at it, working away, trying not to get too bogged down in student life to lose the impetus. Often I was not, and it showed.

'Well you have to keep at it,' he'd reply, with teasing seriousness, 'or you'll never escape the real jobs people expect you to do.'

The second time we met this way, at Stroud railway station, he reached into his pocket and brought out a well-worn wallet.

'Here, have a fiver,' he said, pressing the note on me and leaning in conspiratorially as if Kathy shouldn't hear and couldn't know. 'Go and get drunk and write some POETRY!'

This was not an offer it would have been sensible to refuse, a fiver being quite enough to get drunk on in 1991. I took the money and the advice gladly and headed to the Pelican where all the prettiest women were likely to be drinking, ordered Uley ale and began to write.

Earth Song

Clouds skate over icy skies,
their heavy bellies ready to burst.

The embers of the sun splinter
on distant, claw-like trees

send shards of dank light
tumbling into the valley.

A mob of crows canters into the air
to bully an adventurous owl.

Bluetits pick at the last rotten apple
on an unattended tree.

As shadow swallows the garden
I sit on a log and defy the night.

A bat deftly manoeuvres
through intricate webs of dew-laden pine.

I close my eyes and call your name.
It echoes around the valley,

the sound undulating
through trees and hills,

building power
until my cry is a mantra,

chanted by the whole immediate world
of night creatures, plants and spirits.

I am swallowed whole
by darkness and warmth.

The valley breathes into me
and softly I breathe out your name.

The earth answers in song.
I spin in air currents

as the planet rocks me
in its malleable paw,

croons lullabies and lost odes
in languages I almost understand.

I whisper your name.
The whisper does not vanish,

but is borne on the wings of a butterfly
into the singing storm.

Sun bursts from my pores.
In a fragile case of air I await your reply.

10

The Real Rosie?

Walking out of the cottage and up the airy little path behind the Old Chapel (renamed Scrubs Bottom in a fit of typically British scatological humour) I learned to vanish into the woods to escape homework. I accessed the path by climbing a set of stairs, stairs my father had claimed when they were torn out of the Wilde's cottage in the 1970s and had recycled into a sort of Jacob's Ladder into the woods, a stairway to heaven straight out of *A Matter of Life and Death*, which he would sit on and speak out from like a Beat revolutionary addressing the startled pheasants.

Avoidance of maths took me farther and farther off the beaten track until I rediscovered a small cottage in the heart of the wood, round the corner in the Dillay, that was as close to the style of the cottage I lived in as it had been one hundred years before. Timbercombe Cottage was the home of Rosie Bannen, a warmly welcoming woman of Irish extraction. She had lived in and around the valley since she was a girl, after her father had fled Ireland during the uprising in 1916.

The house was remote – a track rolled down one side of the hill and up the other with no idea of where the road might be – and ran without electricity or water. A telephone had only been put in after

Rosie suffered a heart attack. Walking past, one was greeted by barking and the more distant yowl of cats – Rosie had at least ten cats and an enthusiastic brood of King Charles Spaniels, which would merge into one multi-tongued beast and attempt to lick passers-by to death.

Rosie was as welcoming as her spaniels, albeit in a more civilised manner. The first time I passed, on my own, she hailed me by name, welcoming me back to the valley and keeping me for twenty minutes or more talking about my mother and how she had babysat for me up in Snows Farm when I was a 'tiny golden-haired boy'.

I called by every so often after that for a couple of years (until teenage angst and longing turned me towards the town), intrigued by the rustic life she led in her compact little house, amazed by the clarity of the water she drew from the spring, and overwhelmed by spaniels. She would appear every time subsumed by creatures, sometimes appearing to float over her garden on a tidal wave of cats to offer tea, or perhaps something stronger if my father was there as well – her parsnip and elderflower wine. Her home-brewed valley vintages were good enough to help him overcome his fear of dogs.

Rosie grew into the valley, kept alive by a constant war with the owners of her house, where she was a sitting tenant, and the generosity of friends and neighbours. The owners wanted her out and kept putting up sweetheart deals, demands and obstacles in an attempt to prise her from Timbercombe Cottage. According to Pat Hopf, the track to her house was often blocked so that coal could not be delivered and tractors were left running overnight in an attempt to unsettle her into leaving.

Rosie was having none of it, though – she was a tenacious and hardy woman who thrived on the solitude and the surprise of visitors, walking up to Bisley, three miles away, to do her shopping and keeping shoes in the barn of Norman Williams' farm (the same barn in which I parked my bicycle if I made it up the hill in time for the school bus) so she could change out of her boots if she wanted to head to Stroud dressed up properly for an excursion.

It was considered certain in some circles that this was the Rosie of the cider, of the first promptings of lust that drove Laurie's imaginings and made him sing hymns as he staggered back drunk, late from the haymaking. It seemed too appropriate for her not to be Rosie; time cast a delicate cloak of autumn leaves over Rosie Burdock's shoulders until she became Rosie Bannen, the hale old lady who invited people into her cottage for a drink and regaled them with stories. Time and distance rendered her the likeliest candidate, because she lived a life that was almost as absolutely preserved and quietly iconic as the book that made this valley famous.

If she was, she would not be drawn on the matter – there have been many women ready to lay claim to the title, casting their eyes at willing audiences of tourists and journalists with as much slyness and glitter as they could muster. Rosie Burdock married a soldier. Rosie Bannen would surprise the unwary, assuming her roots to be slow and unwieldy as a beech, with tales of her travels in Turkey and beyond.

It was hard, as a teenager, to imagine her face wrapped in a pulsating haze or her body flickering with lightning, but that was merely the passage of time at play, refining her hefty youthful vigour into a denser shape. The apple of her cheek may have perished, but her white hair curled like an elderflower on her brow and her face was as lined and wholesome as a scrubbed-clean parsnip.

To me she *was* Rosie, the only Rosie the valley allowed, as strong as the cider they sold in the Woolpack, surrounded by cats and spaniels and myth, a ghost of a vanished time who offered me tea and memories the few times I saw her, and who laughed at the hardships placed in front of her as she stomped through the last years of her life in the valley, clinging on as tenaciously as a nettle to the steep banks of the Dillay and doing strategically astute battle with the Social Services, the landlords who wanted to oust her and the steady and increasingly perceptible relentlessness of change.

It doesn't matter, really, who the real Rosie was. An imagined Rosie Bannen, the years shaved from her, will always be the woman I think of as that hefty, terrifying girl tempting Laurie with cider as the haymaking goes on without them a hundred yards away and his brother Jack goes calling his name down the hill.

I walked back to Rosie's cottage last year, in the high spring, as leaf-green clouds began to burst from the bud in the deciduous wood and the rough lane vanished in an atomic haze of growth that had been retarded by a long winter and April frosts. I had not been back for years; Rosie had died whilst I was at college and after my return I had moved into Stroud, had not thought of the depths of the valley, eager to move on and make a life of my own.

What I saw was painful, a stab in the heart of the valley. After Rosie died, the cottage had been left to disintegrate; the last barely changed house in the valley, the one remaining place that had functioned as all these houses had functioned one hundred years ago, was a shell. The slate roof had been lifted off for money and the innards of the house were rotting away, its windows boarded up to hide the desecration. The steep little path to the house, which cut up and down the two sides of the valley, had been crucified by a scar of a lane that had been torn through it to allow easy access for hunters in their four wheel drives, whose raised shooting hides infested the field across from the cottage, where an oak tree shimmered in the late afternoon sun.

It had weathered in, the cottage, on its way to becoming a lost monument like the jawline houses I had played in as a child, nature working its way through it in a toothy enthusiasm of bramble and nettle, the neat patterns of Rosie's garden just visible under their unencumbered growth. The brutal new track had taken on a look of smug permanence that would have fooled anyone walking past it for the first time, but which to me still screamed through the field like a newly opened wound.

I climbed into the house through the broken door, hoping for some sign of survival, but all trace of Rosie was gone. The neat kitchen I remembered was hollow and bird-stained, stove-less and kettle-free, no comfort left. The stairs at the centre of the house would not take my weight; they creaked like a dying animal.

I left, a rush of sorrow tight in my chest, not looking back as I walked up the slippery path and away through the wood to the more familiar emptiness of home.

II

Party Time

As schooldays cycled to a slow, autumnal end, my father spent more time away, working and travelling at weekends. I began to draw friends out by bicycle convoy into the solicitous quiet and freedom of the valley, for parties, for company, for the sake of keeping the house and the valley alive. The house was distant enough from family for there to be no frowning and lectures about smoking or beer or whatever other excess of friendly impairment we could lay our hands on (at least until my father came home and threw his hands up in horror), and for the gang of awkward, clever friends gathered around me to feel free enough to be themselves; they came out there readily, with music and homebrew and everyone carrying something that could be made into food. Free of censure, we drew ourselves inward, fought to make the world that was opening up around us seem safe and small and fun, for a little while.

I bought a moped, purportedly for carrying me ever more swiftly to school but mostly used for winding my way sedately in and out of trouble. A cranky old Honda 50cc, it refused to carry me up the hill out of the valley unless both of my legs were sticking out over the footrests, wading the bike up the hill. I looked, as one unkind observer put it, like a bandy-legged ostrich woefully failing to hurry up. For all its lack of power, it did allow me to pull bicycles up the short, sharp hill heading out of Stroud, reducing the journey time of the convoy by five or more minutes and adding a shiver of danger to the evening. The moped struggled and whined at the extra weight and the bicycles wobbled dangerously as the cyclists clung on to the bar behind the moped seat.

Once we reached the cottage, usually late in the evening on a Saturday, we baked bread and made stew – the contents of visitors' pockets almost always turned up flour and yeast plus a couple of potatoes, carrots, leeks, broccoli – anything that could be thrown in a large pan and cooked with lentils. If the season were right, there'd be nettle heads thrown in as well.

Gaius Moore, the de facto leader of our troupe of friends, was deeply involved in the art of home brewing, and often brought beer and yeast. He also expected that we do something practical, bringing order to evenings that could have quickly and easily degenerated (and sometimes did, regardless) had there not been someone saying: 'Let's bake bread!' And so we boys spilled ourselves drunkenly into the minuscule hours of Sunday mornings, a solid base of rustic foodstuffs well-made and swiftly eaten, loaded afterwards with drink, argument and humour, plus the first murmurings of a fully realised artistic streak amongst our small group.

There was Gaius, or Giz as he was more often known, sharp-witted and satirical, a slyly amused glimmer in his eye, who could often be found dipping into my father's Drambuie in attempted secrecy (which he'd replace and immediately drink again the next time he came out to the valley) when he wasn't calling the next tune on the stereo, demanding with a zealot's grin that Three Card Brag be played or writing sharp, satirical poems. Legzee was almost always found scratching obsessively at the sketchbook he'd bound in leather, which he kept in a handmade leather pouch on his belt. He would get ever more garrulous as the evening wore on and the beer took command and would take to cornering people with long and excited guided tours of his increasingly eccentric and deliriously perverse drawings.

Joe, aggravatingly handsome in waif-thin proto-James Bond mode and yet charmingly uncertain of himself as a teenager, was either drawing or launching into painfully funny improvised satires of friends, enemies, situations – he left us gasping for air, laughing in the smoke-filled cottage, and sometimes a little stung by the unconscious, improvised barbs that occasionally emerged like first wasps from a prodded nest. Euan, by turns taciturn and outrageously blunt, could be relied upon to try things if he was dared to do so. One night someone challenged him to eat a huge clove of garlic in one go – he did, and then yelled like a steam whistle as he let loose the glass in his hand. Euan didn't seem to have moved his arm but the glass, a tough, dimpled half pint tankard, flew across the kitchen and exploded by the window. 'NEVER let me do that *again!*' he said. Everest, a later arrival to the troupe, could usually be found strumming a guitar or pointing a video camera, and was sometimes overwhelmed with a slightly dictatorial take on his own natural ebullience. Matthew Chadwick, genially avuncular even as a teenager, was excited enough by the arcana of science and craft to carry even the gang's most self-consciously arty moods along in his wake.

These parties ceased when I was twenty-one, after a night of mayhem to which it seemed that half of Stroud had come, riding motorbikes across gardens and terrorising the wildlife and not-so-wildlife of the valley. A few of us had set up an artful little system of lights and sound under the canopy of yew, checked that easily excited neighbours were informed or away, made invites with maps, given them out to people we trusted not to share them in the pub, half of whom promptly shared them in the pub. A mellow evening with about forty people turned into a party of one hundred by about 11pm. Cars were littered all over the approach to the valley, motorbikes roared across gardens and tore up precious flowerbeds. Stronger drugs than any of us had anticipated found their way into hands and drinks and mouths, often unnoticed until later, when the night beasts, fields and party people took a distinctly peculiar turn and started to unexpectedly change colour, float above the ground and melt in and out of vision as if they were being animated to the designs of Rothko, Dali and Chagall in trinity. I slipped into unconsciousness in the garden and woke early in bed, uncertain how I'd got there.

In the daze of next morning, with strangers in the front room concocting hash-pipes out of my root vegetable and tinfoil supply behind closed curtains (sat, appropriately, under my father's wall of books by and about the Beat generation), I wandered the house astonished. I was brought sharply and swiftly out of hangover by the arrival of the police, who had been called by a neighbour up in The Scrubs, alarmed enough by the sight of Euan's orange VW Camper Van parked in one of the fields to jump to the conclusion that travellers were invading the valley.

I was standing in the garden contemplating the weakly flashing lights that Matthew Chadwick had erected in the trees when two policemen stepped through the debris, appearing deeply self-satisfied; a look that, combined on both their faces, said: 'we've found ourselves squatters and an illegal rave to liven up this dull Sunday morning.'

'Been having a party, have we?' one of them asked me, sardonically.

'Yes,' I said.

'Got a bit out of hand, did it?'

'Yes, rather,' I said, looking apologetically at the empty cans of beer salting the garden, the motorbikes, the crushed flowers. 'I didn't expect so many people to turn up.'

'And how long have you been living here?'

'All my life,' I replied, deeply thankful that the curtains were closed in the front room.

The policeman drew a disappointed breath and asked my name. I told him.

'You'll excuse us while we confirm this with your neighbours,' he said.

They didn't return.

The real trouble with parties at the cottage was that they rarely included women – except for Kate Lloyd (who had long since let go the affectionate 'y' at the end of her name), Melissa Shaw, Jenny Haigh and a few others, who were either too much like sisters or were too close to us in age to be interested in anything but friendship, the sort of girls who would dismiss one's clumsy overtures with a sharp bark of laughter, a friendly, unresponsive smile and another drink.

Valley and village were both distressingly free of eligible, interested girls – the only ones I knew of were my age and seeing older men, or were older than me. I became painfully aware that, in every direction for a couple of miles, there was no opportunity to forget myself in the arms of someone else, that the houses seemed to be increasingly occupied by retirees and weekenders.

So we banded together and made sure there were parties that women would come to out in the quiet, comforting embrace of Slad, often in the quarry at the side of Swift's Hill, the limestone grassland nature reserve opposite the Woolpack, which is framed to perfection by the pub's windows. We kept absolutely rigidly to the quarry, avoiding the orchids, knapweed and cowslips that fed hosts of butterflies further up the hill. We would secretively haul small sound systems up the slope into the quarry's accidental rococo amphitheatre, light cautious fires and wait, having carefully, carefully put the word out to all the people we could think of who would not in turn invite everyone from the pubs of Stroud and risk a clampdown on these gatherings.

This was the closest we came to post-harvest parties; agriculture had moved on, leaving the valley in its wake. Wheat went down to the whirring tug of the combine harvester and there were too few sheep on the land to require the farmer to ask for help with the shearing. We revelled in it anyway, our weekday schooling and part-time jobs seeming as good an excuse as any to get out into the landscape and celebrate it, and ourselves.

12

Making Music

The Slad Valley at night, away from the cautious hubbub of the Woolpack, is a place of surprise and discomfort. Lit only by the moon or, on a cloudier night, the faint orange glow of Stroud, it is all too easy to quickly leave the comforting proximity of houses and people one knows at least a little and be in dark lanes that end suddenly and which are sound-tracked by explosive night birds, the belligerent rush of hunting badgers and other unnamed, unseen animals whose tracks are obscured but whose breath feels all too close as one stumbles homewards. It is easy to give in to terror, even in a quiet little pocket of Gloucestershire.

Returning to the valley between bouts of university, attempting to settle back in to a quiet life with few neighbours, away from the town, on my own and with nearly all the friends I had acquired at school gone on to cities and lives away from the quietude of country living, I remember panic setting in all too easily once I'd passed Captain George's manorial farmhouse, halfway home from the Woolpack and loaded with beer, aged twenty or so, careering through the cavernous lanes with a badly sung song repeating under my breath to stave off panic. I have ruined too many favourite tunes for myself thanks to a cloth ear and a skinful of panic; the cottage I grew up in, which had been such a haven as a child, feeling far, far away, out into woods encumbered with sallow ghosts and night beasts.

This fear was not helped by a man I met several times on the lanes in twilight, dressed in shabby clothes, whistling more tunelessly than even I could manage in my fear, and wielding a scythe. The first time I passed him, I squeaked a nervous hello, which was met with a grunt and a hard stare. It felt malevolent, and I lived in terror of him and prayed each time I walked home that he would not be on the lane down to Snows Farm. No one I asked knew who he was. Some even suggested I'd seen a ghost of some long-dead worker walking endlessly home.

Of course, the Woolpack was always good for ghost stories. The valley is full of them; they while away the winter, keep little histories and rivalries alive when told, retold and adapted in the safety of a warm bar that's an easy step from home. When you are walking out through the valley alone, they suddenly become all too real in the misty lanes where trees lurch awkwardly at you out of nowhere, caught like giants in the quailing light of a feeble torch, and the mud sucks at your feet down by the perilously narrow Roman bridge.

The huge black dog with red eyes, harbinger of doom and any ailment one could care to invent, was the story that haunted me most. For the best part of a year I took that with me from pub to cottage, hypersensitive with beer and night time solitude. Then, one night, when the moon was a thumbnail sliver in the sky and my torch was flickering right on the edge of battery loss, I caught two flat red orbs in its beam as I stumbled down a steep field, almost home. The light caught a wet, cold spurt of breath rising on the air. There were eyes staring at me out of the dark. I sat down with a bump, convinced by the beer that my end had come, that I was going to be devoured in the dark of the valley just yards from where I had splashed and played as a child.

No prayer came, just panic; a mist of it rising out of me as I sweated on the damp hillside, my backside moist with dew. I sat there for twenty minutes perhaps, although it felt like hours, barely allowing myself to breathe. Finally the black dog of my paranoid imaginings let out a soft moo and ambled away to the stream to drink.

Travelling home became easier after that, terror slithering away into mere aloneness. Easier and yet harder at the same time, as the more I frequented the pub, the more I began to make friends in Slad and find excuses not to be alone.

University finished with, I moved back to the valley full time. All thought of Bisley was left behind (except as a place to collect my dole cheque). I had my sights set solely on Slad. I could not escape the pull of the village, largely thanks to the band two friends had started in college, born out of the extended jams that had spontaneously erupted at parties in houses in the far reaches of the Slad Valley or up on Swift's Hill throughout our teenage years, whipped to a frenzy of eventual tunefulness by drink and quiet experimentation with other, more illicit substances.

Vashty, a name picked at random from the bible and then deliberately misspelled, formalised into an electronica outfit in Sheffield, where its main conspirators, Joe Reeve and Everest Wilson-Copp, were studying art. After college they moved back down to Slad and set up camp in Everest's parents' home, Stroud Slad Farm. The studio was first placed in Everest's small and slope-roofed bedroom, charmingly and entirely dyslexically named 'Cubey Holo', before moving, as the music progressed and Everest's parents saw commercial potential in it, into an outbuilding of the lovingly restored farm that became a soundproofed technological marvel, an exquisite home studio on two floors of an old grain barn.

As the call to music grew in intensity and the quality increased, Stroud Slad Farm became a central hub for inter-generational parties, bringing together disaffected youth with a creative streak, their hippified parents who had made reasonably good on the dreams of a more sustainable sort of wealth and who hadn't quite caved in to the abject capitalist despair of the late 1970s and early 1980s, and all the age-groups in between. Everest's parents had bought the farmhouse as a shell and set up a leather-working business in the grounds whilst they repaired it. It was an ideal moment; a small business blossoming in a valley that had lost its workforce, a valley which needed things to be happening in it again, which was desperate to escape the taint of retirees and commuters that had almost completely sucked the life out of other villages in the area.

The house they created was an exemplar of the sort of country living that wealthy urbanites aspire to now, the sort of home that has property-porn TV presenters salivating openly as they mutter 'location, location, location'; an exquisite old farmhouse brought back from the brink of ruin and laid out in excellent, simple taste, every inch of the building lovingly used and restored. The kitchen was huge, powered by a blazing Aga, which Pauline, the tough little matriarch of the house, rested against constantly, holding court as a seemingly endless stream of zealously outgoing children raced past.

It would have seemed a very male-oriented house had it not been for Pauline, who could quash testosterone-frenzy with one steely glare. The seemingly endless streams of children were, at the core, five sons, of whom Everest was the eldest. Profoundly dyslexic, Everest had developed instead an ear for the textures of music that seemed almost preternatural; he would go into trances in the studio, sometimes assisted, sometimes not, listening with microscopic attention to things the rest of us could not hear. Joe was the melody man, able to tie lyrics into place with a killer tune.

They made a remarkable duo, locked away in their little studio concocting ever more complex music, occasionally inviting others in to work with them: I was often on duty in the first few years of the band as a co-lyricist; Everest's brother David, who looked as if he could have been a Pre-Raphaelite model were it not for the inconvenient fact that he was male, came in to play guitar.

Architects and artists, musicians and farmers came through the doors as the music developed and became more widely known in the crucible of the five valleys of Stroud and I, unable after late nights writing lyrics to stumble the three miles home, would often crash on the sofa, sometimes for days, until asked very nicely and firmly to leave. It became a home away from the increasing isolation of home; the central hub of my Slad Valley, the meeting point between deep rural and urban living.

In Sheffield, Vashty had been producing cutting-edge electronica, utilising the sort of sounds that cropped up in Warp Records' output and, later, in bands such as Underworld, but after returning to the Slad Valley, Vashty's music shifted slowly towards a ruralist, psychedelic, electronically enhanced rock/pop sound, to which I added poetic lyrics in friendly competition with Joe, whose sense of how words could fit with music exceeded my own, and complemented by Everest, whose dyslexia attuned him far more to the sound of the words than the sense and who was a very useful sounding board for poetry as well. The band was completed by Ginny Murray, who had sung with Sailor (most famous for their kitsch hit 'Girls Girls Girls' in the late 1970s), who helped the band slip the leash of its gang-based beginnings and move towards something more elusive and refined.

The trouble was that the music was created in isolation. The songs were fuelled by cycle rides through the countryside and hallucinogenic encounters, technology and small moments of ecstatic wonder, sex and the lack of it, and longing. There was a lot of longing in the music of Vashty. Instead of gigging, the band took their music to parties and tested it out on the willing (and the unwilling, whose opinions were equally useful, if not always so welcome) if they had a stereo system that took cassettes. Joe and Everest bred a certain kind of cool, out of the rat race and high on countryside and isolation from the general run of things, on the beautiful smallness of Slad. It seemed there would be a natural rise, as music and lyrics and sound got better and better, but bands are like soufflé – alter the heat incautiously and everything collapses.

We had all lived too much on top of each other, which didn't help; a small community made smaller by gang mentality. I was in and out of the same people's houses too often for their and my comfort, though I was too lonely to admit that, especially as women began to swirl into the band members' lives, like milk and honey stirred slowly into coffee. We lost ourselves in the countryside as the band created a sound that was different enough to be noticed, fuelled by the sort of outsider sounds that created Trip Hop. Moving away from the urban angst of Portishead and Tricky, Vashty were fusing a rural psychedelic epiphany with sharp lyrics, a cerebral take on rave culture and the sideways pomp of alternative 1980s-vintage pop. There was angst – there's always some form of angst in good pop music, at its best when it is building into something that moves beyond.

It could have worked. They could so easily have grown into something spectacular, reaching up from the steep slopes of Slad to look at the world. The band was signed to a publishing contract by my old neighbour Hugh Padgham, a friend of Ginny's through whom he had heard the music, but Vashty wasn't really ready for the cut and thrust of commercial art. A certain amount of perspective was lost – an internalised expansion that forgot to take into account the clock's need to work with other cogs if it was going to learn to chime.

At the time of signing the contract, I moved on – a part-time lyricist who wasn't particularly musical wasn't really needed in a professional outfit with a publishing deal, especially as their own lyric-writing had improved in leaps and bounds. I wanted more than anything to write poetry, to create my own word music, but I had also been put on my guard when arguments broke out about who had written what song. Worst of all, I found myself defending my right to a forlorn love lyric, written entirely on my own and for which there was no way I was going to cede any credit to Everest, who was suspecting, wrongly, that his role in the band was at risk.

Within a year Vashty was gone – another band that might have been (and should have been, listening back now to the tapes I've saved, divorced from nostalgia and with the appraising ear of someone who has listened extensively to a wide range of the music that came after) if only it had been set up as an equal partnership. Another cottage industry lost in a place that had been slowly and surely stripped of all such things; the band's implosion drove me further from the valley, out into life and work, believing that I could not find creative satisfaction so closely locked to home.

13

Cannabis with Rosie

After I came back from university and was a little more able to look after myself, my father came back less and less from London, taking up urbanity again with what seemed to me a small sigh of relief, though a green and pollen-scented cloud of fond nostalgia for the valley, and for the years of my paradisal childhood spent there together, under the watchful, loving eye of my mother, hangs unshifting and warm in his heart to this day.

I bought a motorbike, in a bid to survive and be free to travel, and roared around the five valleys of Stroud on it, singularly failing to find any work, whether through indifference or lack of skills. I still have, somewhere, a letter from the local garage telling me that I didn't have what it took to be a garage attendant. Although they phrased it more delicately than that, it was enough to confound the dole office for a while.

I picked up moments of work; Ginny, who sang with Vashty, was married to a sheep farmer, David Murray. David had need of help with the dipping of sheep and I was called in. They lived in a barn on the edge of Sheepscombe and Painswick, which was being slowly converted for home living over at least a decade. When I first encountered the place, the bathroom was hidden behind a curtain

and required careful negotiation at parties if one didn't want to burst in on people unannounced.

Unprepared, but willing to throw myself at anything for money, I made my way up to the farm. All I really knew of sheep was that they looked like small, greasy clouds in a field from a distance and had strange and difficult eyes when you looked at them closely. The closest I had come to a sheep previously was when, as a child, I had been taking turns with Skanda to look out over the fields through new binoculars from my bedroom window. We spotted an unmoving sheep and went to investigate. Close to, it was clear that it was dead – the sheep's corpse was alive with maggots, undulating through its exposed bones like dead grass in a high wind. We ran home, excited and horrified, carrying the stench in our teeth, and helped make the report to the farmer, our details breathy and tangled, spilling out disorderly into the phone.

I got to know sheep a little better than I had bargained for that summer morning in David Murray's field. Crammed with them into a maze-like pen, forcing them through a series of gates leading to a concrete vat, which had been dug into the field and was awash with organophosphates, every detail of them was exposed: the greasy roughness of their wool, hung with dirt and faeces; the horrified, concentrated fury in their eyes. The sheep smelled of shit and fear close up, and battered against me as I tried to ease them towards the vat, wriggling in my arms and bleating angrily as they sank into the murky chemical bath.

The summer sun beat down on me like a fist and the acrid stench of sheep and dip clawed at my nostrils. David, used to his beasts and their maniacal refusal to submit, called encouragement to me and cheerful insults to them. I was quite startled by the way the sheep tried to climb up me like large, aggressive beetles, pummelling their hooves against my chest, their mad eyes staring horrified into mine. The beauty of the Sheepscombe Valley and the heat of the sun were forgotten; all I wanted was to get the job done and get out.

I became clumsy with exhaustion as the day wore on, unused to the intensity and physicality of the work of hefting sheep into the dip. Finally, one animal caught me off balance, barging into my legs to get away. I was knocked sideways, plunged one leg into the rancid vat of chemicals before I could right myself. Unprotected, organophosphates soaked straight through my jeans, sousing my leg. I swore copiously and vowed not to work with sheep again. We finished the day's work. Within six months, as a consequence of this exposure and my erratic approach to healthy living, I had succumbed to pneumonia, numerous calamitous losses of balance resulting in deep cuts to my arms, and a blood clot in my dip-soaked leg.

The motorbike had other uses. One summer party up at the Murray's, before the dipping incident, it was brought out and used to race around the unsown outskirts of a field of hay, bike helmets forgotten. David only issued one stern warning: 'Don't ride into the hay.' Various people took the bike out, riding around the field two at a time. I took advantage of my ownership and offered rides to the girls, whether or not their boyfriends were clamouring to take the bike for a spin. The third time round the field, carrying one pretty, dark-haired girl on the back, the bike skidded and she and I fell, laughing, to the floor, buried in the field's golden fringe.

Laughter slowed to longer consideration of one another, but the moment was shattered when her boyfriend came charging through the centre of the field, insisting that it was his turn on the bike, effectively ending all such games by flattening a diagonal stripe through the hay.

The motorbike was the last thing keeping me in the valley, a bridge between the slow rustic life and the very-faint-but-still-compelling 'urban' throb of Stroud. London had never been an option – exciting to visit and instantly overwhelming, I could not stay more than a week without craving the ability to vanish into the woods, to separate myself from people. On the motorbike, I felt connected. I could get in and out of town in fifteen minutes; I was free to visit friends.

One friend lived in the heart of Slad, in a small house on the way home from the Woolpack with a caravan in the back garden. I had stayed in that caravan often, too out of it to walk the two miles home. This was either thanks to the extraordinary strength of the beer at the Woolpack (Pigs Ear and Old Spot from Uley Brewery –

two beers that will creep up on you in a dark country lane and knock all sense from you a good half-hour after you've finished drinking, the taste of malt and hops lingering on your tongue like a kiss), or because my friend, 'John', grew skunk weed in vast quantities in the spare room of his tiny cottage.

In any small community without work, ways of alleviating boredom will always be sought, and this was my generation's – no cider behind the hay bales for us; we had cannabis with Rosie and what few hay bales were still left in the fields floated by in hallucinatory parade. Skunk creeps into your bloodstream carrying explosives, lifts the roof from your skull, breathes fire in your lungs and spins a bondage rope of speechless wonder and terror around your tongue. It made it difficult to commune with one's intended Rosie when inhaling it, made me master of the foolish amorous giggle, the laugh that thrives without words but thinks it speaks volumes. It once convinced me that a university friend of Kate Lloyd's whom I had tried and failed to woo was in psychic communication with me across the valley. It made a liability of the best of us.

It certainly made motorbiking dangerous. Always careful not to drink and drive, I was less than cautious with skunk and found myself incautiously drifting across the road numerous times as I attempted to head home from John's, giddy with the excitement of speed. One night I only pulled myself together as I was slowed by the scrape of wall on footrest. I had risen onto the pavement and was drifting into the low dry-stone wall that separated the road from the hill down to the stream that cuts through Slad. I would have plummeted headlong into an uncaring field of sheep had I not braked and turned.

The night the motorbike's headlight failed, I was halfway down the road to Stroud. Stopping to assess my options, I was profoundly glad to be in a landscape that had cradled me almost from birth. I had just enough light to see by; there was a bright summer moon, nearly full, pouting at the lip of the hill, spilling a milk-silver sheen on the road. I had just begun to head cautiously home when a police car passed me in the other direction. Brain pickled, a sudden surge of panic rising in my chest and riding a bike that wasn't roadworthy, I heard them slow and turn. I revved the bike hard and roared off, keeping what little light that still emanated from the headlight tight on the road's white lines, listening intently to the siren rising and closing like the opening of a punk record over the pounding rhythm of my heart. I careered off to the left at the Vatch, squealing round the sharp corner and down into the twisting lanes that led to Swift's Hill, Elcombe and, eventually, home.

I had a good head start, but the police were persistent. They had to slow down on the lanes and could not track my exact whereabouts easily, but they kept up a close pursuit on the single lane, follow-ing hard behind as I wove through looming hedgerows and rattled over the cattle grid below Swift's Hill, slowing a little to be sure I'd hit it at the right angle and wasn't going to suddenly pitch forward into the road, skidding on grit patches in the centre of the lane as I braked. I could feel the police continually catching up like an itch in my spine, and revved up the hill to Elcombe, suddenly realising in a flush of relief how I might be able to get away. This was a game of owl and mouse, and I needed to do as mice do, to freeze and hide.

Dipping down from Swift's Hill and revving up to the top of Elcombe, round the Y curve of the valley, looking over my shoulder and catching glimpses of Slad's tiny specks of orange and white, I came to John Papworth's old house, Rose Cottage (owned at the time by the painter Oliver Heywood). Perched at the edge of the woods and below the long, steep and winding hill up to Catswood, it was the perfect place to vanish. I had known it for so long. I shot into the woods along the green lane that opened by the cottage, trav-elling as far along it as I dared, with little light now to see by as trees began to curve in and crop out the moon. Fifty yards in, I skidded to a halt in a patch of cow parsley, killed the engine and what remained of the lights.

I threw myself to the floor, panting and trembling with adrena-line, counting on the police to assume that I had continued up the hill, which I could have done easily without them seeing any trace of me through the dense woodland. Within a minute I saw their lights flickering blue through the trees, the sirens bouncing waspish from the hill as they pelted nearer, shot by, slowed for the extended S bend and kept on going. I waited a few minutes and began to pick myself back up again, celebrating my good fortune. I was too quick

to celebrate – just as I was mounting the bike and raising my foot to the kick-start, ready to take the long way home through Stroud, there was the sound of a car coming down the hill.

I paused, peered through the woods to the bare tarmac knuckle of the hill. The car slowed and drew to a halt outside Rose Cottage. Doors opened and two voices cut through the night.

'D'you think he went into the woods?' said one.

'Could be,' said the other. 'He seemed to know this lane well enough and it looked like a trail bike.'

'Worth taking a look?'

'No, he'll probably be vanished into Stroud by now.'

A torch flashed through the undergrowth, some yards from where I stood, frozen between terror and relief that my motorbike was entirely black (apart from a white skull and crossbones on the front, which I instinctively covered with my hands). Eventually the policemen gave up, got into their car and drove off slowly down the lane. They seemed to take hours leaving. My heart skittered like an insect caught under glass, until finally I worked up the courage to kick down and jolt the bike to life again, trembling slowly up the lane to home, adrenaline and sweat cold on my back, remembering my mother's 'strange reluctance to enter within doors'.

The bike didn't last much longer; without work I couldn't afford its upkeep or insurance. I took it off the road and sold it for far less than I'd paid, packed up my books and clothes and left the valley for Stroud, away from isolation, constant effort and the pervasive, hazy memories of childhood ease.

14

Not Available

In memory, cherished by dream, a landscape of any stripe stays the same as it was when you last lived in its depths, romanticised by longing, by the desire to return. Leaving the cottage, I was almost immediately consumed by that longing, but only returned out of necessity, to switch the heating on and off with the seasons or to collect my father's post when he was away too long.

As a child, the valley had seemed mine in its oracular completeness. As an adult, outside the swaddling fields, I began to discover that many other people felt the same and, more importantly, how deeply they felt that connection with Slad and its surroundings. I read *Cider with Rosie* for the first time in my mid-twenties, having reasoned unreasonably as a teenager that I had no need to do so. I knew the stories, didn't I? They had passed into local legend. I'd lived that life, hadn't I? As a child and a teenager I had grown up at the bosom of that book, surely.

I was wrong, of course; Laurie Lee's experience of a life long gone, at the edge of the modern age when cars were no more than a distant rumble, when only the rich could afford to sit in the road and dreamily mutter 'Poop poop' in the manner of Mr Toad, was far removed from mine. Laurie's countryside was filled with people piled up on top of one another, in small houses where children shared rooms, pressed into four walls, crushed together and rarely leaving the square mile they lived in, living more often than not without concentrated thought of anywhere else, except occasionally, in the abstracted form of newspapers or the more concrete, unpublishable forms of news brought through by wandering escapees from other lives.

I realise how free I was, how liberated and how lonely, in that little cottage with only the valley and an occasional friend to play with; how I had built the valley around me as less of a cocoon, more as an invisible shell that I could take with me whenever I left. What I didn't quite realise was how likely it was to change. Looking at photographs of the valley as it was one hundred and more years ago, the places I knew as dense woodland were treeless, the cottages stark against the hill. Even in my short childhood it was changing rapidly, as the recently installed lines of power and communication opened up the valley to the world. Nature gets on with things almost unnoticed, especially if all that you are concentrating on is yourself.

In the first year or so away from the valley, it was easy – constant access to a social calendar revolving around the pubs I worked in, the cafés I frequented and the poetry gigs I sought out further afield made for what seemed like a busy life. In the mid 1990s, however, Slad came under threat from housing development and I developed a series of nightmares about the valley; cinematic, hyper-realistic dreams that recur to this day in which every corner of the landscape is bricked over and all that is left of the old valley is the Woolpack, with a big neon sign over it flashing the words 'Laurie Lee drank here' into the night.

Fortunately, Laurie was in a mood to defend the valley ferociously, despite illness and near blindness. A series of meetings were set up, at which Laurie sat in, totemic, his hands on his stick in a quietly combative pose, making statements like: '[The Slad Valley is] the green lung of Stroud. If we permit this to go ahead without resistance, it will be a self-inflicted wound that not even time will heal. The word 'development' is just a euphemism for ravagement and exploitation ... The valley, with its landscape of tangled woods and sprawling fields, should be left to rabbits, badgers and old codgers like me.'[1]

It wasn't just old codgers that took up the defence of the valley from exploitation, or wanted to be a part of it, though. Poets and artists, walkers and drinkers, locals and tourists all cried for Slad to be spared – the valley turned out to be everyone's valley and I, as vocal in its defence in and around Stroud as I could manage, discovered and rediscovered a huge number of people who would gladly call it their own.

Carolyn White, who had spent winters in Driftcombe painting the sprawling fields and tangled woodlands in all their stark glory when I was a teenager, had put down her flag in the landscape with brutal expertise. She became more and more widely noticed for her broad impressionist take on Slad, fixing it further in the mind's eye as somewhere of special note. She returned often to the valley, always finding something new to paint, some new way to look at light. When I encountered her in Stroud talk would routinely return to that landscape, the feel of it, the people in it and sometimes the parties she'd held in Driftcombe that I had come to. She remembered me running from one of these when Rich, a year or two younger than me and the son of one of her friends, proposed holding a séance in the most haunted parts of the house. The spirit apparently in attendance was female and her name began with an F. Having lost my mother, Frances, only a couple of years before, I jumped from the board and ran, taking my father's midsummer jogging route in reverse, and at full pelt, all the way home.

Carolyn's canvases became more and more like stained glass; she caught the valley at its richest and coldest, always making it sing with light. She was a short and intense woman, her rounded, good-natured face hiding fierce eyes and a sharp opinion of poets ('It's all very well to write poetry, Adam; just don't become one of those types who won't help a person push a stuck car up a hill because "it's not the sort of thing a poet does!"'). She could often be found wandering the valley carrying easel and paint, chasing the sun.

---

1 Grove, Valerie, *Laurie Lee: The Well-Loved Stranger*, p. 500.

The only time she encountered Oliver Heywood, equally a master of capturing the valley in light, was near Rose Cottage in Elcombe. They were coming through the woods in opposite directions, carrying recognisably similar equipment; both had spent years combing the valley for places to stop and paint and yet they only met that once, pausing to make small talk and recognise each other as artists before moving on, interested more in the valley itself than in one another, and never, apparently, to meet again.

There, still defending the valley in her own quiet way, was Diana Lodge, capturing details of the valley where Carolyn and Oliver's work looked at broader landscapes. In her late eighties she was still producing many dozens of paintings a year and selling them at the Stroud Subscription Rooms for charity, but she had weathered ever further into the landscape, driving erratically between Slad, Stroud and Prinknash Abbey.

But it was Laurie's voice that mattered most in the battle to protect and protest. Laurie, in cahoots with Val Hennessey, concocted a defence of Slad against development for the *Daily Mail*, a story which reached out across Britain and the world, particularly to Japan and America. A tidal wave of protest came rushing back, from people who loved *Cider with Rosie*, who loved the valley or their imagined version of it, giving the landscape a loud and unanimous voice against the steady spread of tarmac and flood risk, the twin erosions of soil and hope.

The next year, Laurie died. Although Slad was safe for a while and free to allow the creep of small creatures, old codgers and unfettered leaf-light through its scattered fields and woods, the rush of hope returned to a trickle and my dreams of houses walking in on chicken legs and colonising the valley returned. I saw them strutting and scratching through Slad as if they had wandered out of some Russian fairytale, before settling on all the beloved places I had known.

At the time I was writing poetry for performance, invective in verse; nightmares and poems naturally spilled over into one another. In one: 'They bought the woods above Slad/and are erecting a wicker Laurie Lee/to burn houses in: hot living for the millennium.' In another, the nightmares went beyond millennial frenzy and imagined a dystopian Slad:

At This Time

Statistics; not available.
Plans and applications; not available.
Photocopied reports from bloody depths of bureaucracy;
                                        not available.

Orchards; not available.
Aspirin; not available.
Pleasant valley walks; not available.
Childhood available elsewhere.

Sunday school; not available.
Imagination; not available.
Cider presses; not available.
Big dogs with grotty noses; not available.
Kissing gates; not available.
Beer; not available.
Reporters only available if beer available.

Books; not available.
Economists; not available.
Bare-footed taxmen no longer available.
Miffed of Miserden; not available.
Sculptors; not available.
Cowslips; not available.
Pools to drown in; not available.
Sewage and concrete available always
if price is right.

Prices; not available.
Wallets; not available.
Poets and anarchists not available
except for lecture tours in far countries
with big wars.
England wicket keepers; not available.
Trees; not available.
Sunsets; not available.

Badgers not available unless peanuts paid for.
Bungalows available at all times.

Pig-farmers; not available.
Sheep; not available.
Locals not available for comment or otherwise.
Telephones available, but not as available as vandals.
Chaffinches; not available.
Torches not available or necessary.
Bicycles; not available.

BBC film crews and other archaeologists; available.
Holographic Laurie Lee; available.
Midsummer morning traffic-log; available.
Small chunks of Cotswold stone; available.
Mortgages; available.
Rustic 1930's charm available
from staff of three-story theme restaurant
        on request.
Chartered helicopter flights; available.
Genuine gravestones; available.

'Cider with Disney'; available.
Sex in aforementioned bungalows; available.
Prices available for that.
Prime Minister available for facile speeches
about importance of countryside
and visits from Presidents

Jilly Cooper; available.
Jilly Cooper; available.

Explosives not available.

At
this
time.

15

Burials

Death is an implosion; a sucking away of memory, a shrivelling of fact until it is indivisible from myth. In the summer of 1995, Marcelle Papworth, the wife of John, died. The Papworths had long ago left the valley, but they owned some of the woodland behind the house, and John wanted Marcelle to be buried there. Approval was sought, and was only granted after strenuous debate, according to the nature of bureaucracy in small areas of outstanding natural beauty.

The location of the grave site was far off the beaten track, on a little hillock that catches the sun through the trees late but not too late on a summer's day, in amongst the ruins of a more crowded century. Earth had silted up over fading walls, moss-encrusted semi-structures so embraced by root and soil that it is hard now to tell if they were once houses or merely garden or animal enclosures. The only way to reach it is to walk, or park precariously on the steep and slithering S bend – the lane barely allows for cars to pass and the green lanes through Catswood are only good for hiding motorbikes or riding horses.

Granted the right for a woodland burial, and the ground consecrated, the Papworths then found themselves without a digging

crew. First, the pub was tried. Eventually phone calls were made to Diana Lodge, many of whose grandchildren were in the valley at the time, and she sent Brodie, Caitlin and Owen along to help dig. It was hard, rocky ground and a hot summer; more hands were needed. I was called in, along with Euan, to help make the work go faster.

Every step down through the hill was layered with stone and mud, bonded together into a kind of gristle, tough and impenetrable. The Lodges had got a couple of feet in before Euan and I arrived. They were desperately in need of a rest. We took it in turns with a pickaxe and shovel, smashing through layers of the past, throwing out small animal skulls we'd crushed, yanking at roots, our fingernails filthy, gloves forgotten, blisters rising on our hands, watching worms writhe back the way they had come after finding their usual routes exposed. The task began to seem impossible, so the work party turned to laughter and beer as it dug, determined not to let this armoured skin of stone defeat us. Old stories of childhood, jokes and songs, tender insults and harsh encouragement flew back and forth across the deepening grave; anything to distract us from the impossibility and the enormity of the task, the responsibility of it.

As the day wore on and we wore out, new fervour came over Euan (ever the man to stare defeat in the face, snarl '*Yew*'ve *GOT* to be *KIDDING* me!' and plough on regardless, whether it was playing golf on the Sega Megadrive until six in the morning or digging an impossible grave). He pummelled away at the hole, getting deeper and deeper into the ground as the sun sank into the opposite hill, trailing a coat of honey down the fields. Sometimes he wouldn't even let others take over and carried on hammering, a fierce look in his eyes, only stopping to let people in so that they could clear the debris he had created.

Between us we made it before sunset, got as close to six feet deep as we could, with more than enough stone dug up to discourage any animal from digging down through it when it was replaced. We went to the Woolpack to celebrate.

'What've you been doing?' we were asked.

'Digging a grave in Elcombe,' we replied. There was much muttering in the pub.

The funeral itself is a hazy memory, blocked out by mists of hangover and the previous day's hard work. We diggers were there, all salt, cynicism and mordant laughter from the strain of the dig long left behind. John, caught between liturgical ecstasy and grief, stood at the head of the grave like a woodland god in priest's robes, filling the wood with his voice and with the memory of Marcelle.

Three years later, I was in the Woolpack having a drink with Everest. Janette, living with him in the village at that time, and working in the pub kitchen, finished her shift and came to join us.

'Have you heard about the grave in the woods above Elcombe?' she asked me.

'Mmm,' I replied, sipping my pint.

'Martin was telling me about it,' she continued, a glimmer of disapproving excitement in her eyes. 'It was years ago. Apparently this man came in and wanted help digging a grave for his wife. Nobody would do it! They all said it was too stony. But there's a grave there now. Isn't that weird?'

'How long ago was this?' I asked.

'Maybe thirty years ago,' said Janette. 'It's weird. Why would someone do that?'

'I helped dig that grave,' I said. 'A couple of years ago.'

'I don't believe you,' said Janette.

BURIALS

I remember you telling me
of a burial years ago in Elcombe woods
up at the high point, the stony point
where local workmen
chewing their cud of cider
refused to work.
They told the husband that his wife
would get no further down
than three feet, you said,
although the grave was eventually dug.

You seemed astonished,
questioned the sanctity of such an act
siding in Protestant horror
with the old rogues buried in their pints
who mix and match their myths to suit the night.
You closed off when I told you I had dug the grave
with the family of the deceased two years before,
had stood, at six foot four, shoulder deep
in consecrated earth,
carving out a fragment of the hill.

It was as if I disappointed you,
gave you a truth you did not need
intruding on your tale with pick and spade.
All stories tell truths. I know that now.
Unwritten memories and bodies
subside like pit villages
but they leave small spaces
where poppies and dandelions grow
amongst resurgent grass.
All burials are beginnings.

By 1998 all three of the points on the asymmetrical diamond of connection that had brought my parents to the edge of Slad had gone. Laurie had been feted and celebrated after his death quite as much as he had been before – the valley held on to him as firmly and lovingly as he had held onto it in all the years he had spent in Spain and London. Diana Lodge died peacefully the following year and was honoured with a funeral parade through Stroud before being buried at Prinknash Abbey.

I too had left, though I had not travelled far. My father spent more and more time in London. Our cottage stood empty too much of the time, inhabited only by the gentle, faded presence of my mother as we remembered her and my father's cornucopia of fading papers and unmoved books. Like a castle in a fairytale, the cottage began to be buried by its surroundings, a sleeping beauty lingering deep within the encompassing thorns.

16

Beginnings

I magine again, if you will, bicycles being steered through a long, ungainly line of cars parked on the road; the concerned lights blinking sleepily on in the old schoolhouse as the bicycle riders on The Night of a Thousand Laurie Lees cruise and curse, topple and laugh at the clumsiness of their arrival. Imagine their bicycles parked hugger-mugger against the solid metal fence, placed there to keep drunkards from falling into the beer garden, wheels tangled with pedals, feet and brambles.

Without Laurie there, feeling his way through the valley and dishing out advice, flirtation and impish misdirection to passers-by in equal measure, without his spirited public persona coalescing constantly into the foreground, Slad changed. Money came dancing in; house prices soared. It became a place of aspiration and excitement. Strange things were afoot in the valley, as if one thousand Laurie Lees really had come stumbling through the valley signing any book they had to hand and had cast a spell on the landscape.

It was difficult at times to spot these changes – at one point, a young man moved to the village, claiming he was an antique dealer. He lived in a grand house, part of the Squire's old estate, at the bottom of the hill on Steanbridge Lane, with his partner and

her small daughter. Nobody really paid them much mind – they seemed together, enough part of the new landscape of Slad to be left alone. They were antique dealers and hadn't antique dealers been plying their trade round here for years? They paid their rent. They seemed likeable enough, though he was off travelling with work and she was often flaked out. Visiting friends in the converted stables next door, all I could see was that the daughter was lonely and rather more attached to my friends than might be considered usual, these days at least, but which seemed to me not to be too unusual for village life.

My friends used to take the daughter in and look after her, concerned that she wasn't getting enough attention. They'd tell her stories and get her painting. They'd take her for walks along the lane, past the lake where someone had drowned herself eighty years before and which I had found to my horror to be full of medicinal leeches when I went fishing there with Katy Lloyd as a child. I came out of the lake white-faced and trembling, my bamboo fishing net blurring in my hand, with at least five leeches attached to my limbs. Alan Lloyd whipped out a cigarette, lit it and burned them until they shrivelled and fell from my skin like bloodied scabs. I stood there wide-eyed with shock, Katy laughing at me, sluiced with pondweed and water.

A couple of months after the antique dealer moved in, a policewoman moved into the other converted stable and things began to get a little weird. The antique dealer and his partner became elusive, the daughter visited my friends more often and an atmosphere of tension descended on the quiet little cluster of houses. Within a few weeks the dealer was under arrest, having been found to be dealing in things far less bulky and far more lucrative than antiques, and to be carrying a decidedly new sawn off shotgun to assist him in doing business.

Drugs weren't new to the village of course; a large section of Slad's teenagers knew my house not because they knew me as such but because, when cattle were still being kept on the fields below me, the finest psilocybin-laced fungi in the area grew there. Pale-eyed foraging teenagers, kneeling on hassocks of grass in the marshier areas of pat-strewn turf, could be easily startled come autumn if one merely shouted hello to them across the field. Like foxes they would blink and scatter, coming back to the good picking grounds when danger had passed.

Drugs are an easy means of escape in a small village (where borders are wide and horizons distant if you don't have the money to reach them) but they are difficult to support as a cottage industry. My friend 'John', sole carer for his small son, grew too ambitious and filled his spare bedroom with hydroponics to grow cannabis, row upon row of fat resinous green fists bursting from stems, because he was unable to find work that kept the wolf from the door and allowed his son to be looked after. He grew lonely, and the circle of friends he allowed into his secret world of ridiculously lucrative lamp-lit fecundity bloated to unsafe proportions. There were far too many of us coming in to play guitar or computer games, talk, argue and laugh the night away or amble down to the Woolpack to nurse a pint and play pool in the chilly cellar.

It was the talk of Slad for a few days when the police came raiding, taking away lights and plants: 'Did *you* know what was going on?' 'How long has he been doing *that* for d'you think?' 'What will happen to the little boy?' Someone had snitched, and John lost everything except his son and his freedom. Eviction from Slad was punishment enough.

As the village changed, so too did the pub. Rough-hewn and unmodernised, it was a place of safety for many characters and genial reprobates. Big-bearded Martin, who when he was not drinking worked with pigs, was the soul of the pub, part of the fixtures and fittings. I would see him every time I went in, a pint of cider clamped in one hand and a roll up permanently peering out from beneath his moustache. He would sit at the end of the bar, under the till, immovable as stone, a canny look in his eye and a smoker's laugh on his lips. He was taken by mouth cancer eventually, the roll ups and the cider boiling on his tongue for years in lethal combination, but was such a well-loved presence that a portrait of him still hangs laughing over his old seat. So rumour has it, Laurie would invite him and others back to his house after hours and feed them whiskey in exchange for helping him sign books. Pub culture always brews such rumours.

It seemed that, as soon as my father and I were absent more often than not from our quiet corner of the Slad Valley, new life began to creep back into the valley. Mrs Bevan's excitingly derelict little cottage was repaired and extended by her granddaughter Sally Rees who, with her husband Neil, turned the haunted-seeming little cave of Cotswold stone which had hidden a horde of cats into a palace made of the same materials as the original house – it would have looked as if it had been there for centuries when they finished, were the stone not so clean and bright.

After them came the McCroddans, occupying the old Lloyd house, Hugh Padgham having moved over the valley into the heart of Slad. Both households started families and the valley became almost as lively a place as it had been when I was a child. I visited occasionally, to make sure the house was as up together as an empty house can be, to see that the water was off in the winter and the heating was on at a gentle quiver to stop it degrading and being buried completely.

I took girlfriends out there, keen to show them that this was the root of me, to inculcate them in the myths of my youth. The first woman I took, Callie, looked at it and me with sad, hard eyes, not really wanting to know it seems to me now. We lay instead in a cloud of birdsong and cowslips in the field above the Roman bridge, dancing round the edges of sex like bees after nectar, alighting delicately in different places. Not far distant enough from the path, we were interrupted by walkers. They laughed at us, shouted ribald greetings as they passed.

The supposedly Roman bridge had apparently been hacked down to size a century before by two old ladies up at Snows Farm who objected to carriages coming past them on the way to Bisley, and objected to the way the drivers peered over the wall and invaded their privacy. Without the bridge, trade through the valley died out – it had once housed a pub and many more houses and there had even been a brothel on the hill above the Dillay – and we were left to birdsong and the wolf-whistling of walkers.

As time went on and the house stood emptier and sadder, I stopped taking girlfriends and went less and less myself, unable to bear it. The house faded, became more and more a mausoleum to my mother, the wild of the valley choking out the sound of Blake's innocent pipes that we had played in the valley in my youth. Only birds and insects piped down the valley in anything but memory.

17

The Buddha of Swift's Hill

Mecca for butterflies feeding on upright bromegrass and violets, the nectar of black knapweed; livid with rare musk and frog orchids, alongside their hardier companions; occasional home of sacred cows, munching down the grass to let these rare plants grow. Swift's Hill: home of walkers and love-makers, gentle parties and solstice gatherings, high enough to see all the way west to Wales, the broad bosom of the Black Mountains misty over the Severn's glittering steel. Swift's Hill, the high mountain of Slad, where the gods settle and discuss the doings of the day.

One morning a thirty-foot Buddha appeared on Swift's Hill, out of nowhere, perched in clear view of the road and framed to perfection in the Woolpack's window behind the bar. It appeared from a distance to have grown up out of the hill, birthed from the delicate genitalia of an orchid perhaps. It sat there smiling, seraphic, offering benefaction and content. It shocked passers-by, this strange manifestation, brought wagging tongues together in happy dishar-mony in the pub, invigorated newspapers. No one could be certain where it had come from. Theories spread like dandelion seeds, blowing up and down the valley and eager to take root.

I cycled up to the hill with friends, determined to see it for myself before it vanished again, or was removed. We climbed the hill, puffing up past the Vatch and dumping our bikes in the parking space at its foot. Above us, the Buddha loomed genially, shut-eyed and enormous in a crook of the hill. We scrambled up to it, gasping irreverently for breath on the steeper sections, slipping forward and grasping handfuls of turf to steady the climb, trying not to disturb the plant life too much in our eagerness to see.

Close to, the Buddha sported dark lines at regular intervals up his body. It was clear suddenly that he came in sections, and must usually lurk elsewhere, in chunks, easily stored and out of sight unless required for sudden manifestations and celebrations. It was not immediately clear what his presence was celebrating that day, so we admired him a little longer and went freewheeling back to the pub to listen to the speculations, the laughter and the discontent.

A litany of opinions roiled around the pub: 'It's amazing! I love it.' 'It's rude is what it is. That's a nature reserve. It could be doing untold damage.' 'I think it's lush.' 'What would Laurie Lee think?' 'Who cares?' 'Laurie would have loved it. I love it.' 'It's stupid. Who's got that sort of time to waste?'

Hours were wasted with the thrill of the Buddha of Swift's Hill, whether it was approved of or not. It brought the local papers running, ever eager for something new and strange to write about, caught in the permanent trap of an endless small community slow news day. Myths sprang from the tongues of locals, all of us ready to expound on whimsical theories through a filter of alcohol. I told anyone who would listen (and not too many did, given that they had theories of their own) that it had belonged to Laurie Lee and that he had asked friends to erect it as a constant reminder that the valley was a sacred space.

It was fanciful, but then the valley allowed for flights of fancy, encouraged them and let them grow if they were strong enough. It does not seem far-fetched at all that there might be some presiding spirit looking out from under its green skin. 'As sure as God's in Gloucestershire,' the saying goes. That may be true, but in Slad the closest one gets to gods are people who have imprinted themselves on the landscape, hardy presences born of toil or art that shift and change, decay and are revived.

One can see the bones of them in the crooked walls of Cotswold stone that line the roads in ever fainter procession out of Slad, absorbed by fence lines and scrabbling hedgerows, dark wet moss coating them for their last winters as they fail to be repaired. The past is a book laid out in pages of divided fields, should one care to read them; a book that becomes harder to read as people cull its pages for other books, cut them up and sample them. Words and actions thread through the valley like teased wool, binding the past and present together, inseparable. Standing astride both ancient and modern eras is Laurie, and the memory of him, bound up in the valley, preserving and preserved by it, too much a human being to ever risk becoming a god.

After three days the Buddha vanished, leaving a sudden vacuum for other myths and gossip to rush towards and fill. No lasting mark was left by its absence; people quickly forget novelty when there is the day-to-day beauty of life in the summer abundance of Slad to take its place. It is easy to forget when there are long grasses to lie in whilst the sun shines, a beer garden to occupy as the last light of evening falls in a halo on Swift's Hill.

The image of the Buddha still lingers in my eye, though; as does the knowledge that somewhere, not far away, a man with an impish smile guards its sections undercover in his garden, laughing still at the reactions to his prank.

18

Notting Hill in Wellies

As all things change, so too the Woolpack changed. Dave, the genial crumpled landlord, purveyor of fine beers and quick food, decided it was time to sell. The village became overnight a riot of panicked whispers and morbid speculations as to who might take his place. The village's breath shortened as its alcohol-laced heart skipped a few beats. Who could replace Dave and his convivial, old-fashioned set-up? The pub had stocked papers and sent teenagers out on paper rounds on his watch and was always a gently welcoming place, unless it was the height of tourist season and was painfully full of walkers.

What if it were taken over by a pub chain and became the sort of bland everypub that had begun to infest the towns and villages of Britain, where everything from the beer to the beer mats was exactly the same and music and food was piped at the customer at a level just low enough to irritate? Worse, what if it were to close and leave the village with only a road packed with cars rushing through, no one finding a need or having a reason to stop?

Turmoil and angst flooded the fields and would have surely caused the stream to burst its banks had Dan Chadwick not stepped in and bought it. Youngest son of the sculptor Lynn, who had come

to Gloucestershire after meeting Diana and Oliver Lodge, Dan was the perfect person to take on the pub. He was part of the imagined landscape of Slad, an artist in his own right living over the hill at Lypiatt Park and sweeping down for a drink at the Woolpack on a regular basis. He knew the locals. The locals knew him. The pub loved him and he loved the pub.

Dan's intervention was a velvet revolution for the Woolpack. Everything changed and nothing did. It was retrofitted to look older than it was, craftsmen rolling in to make brand new ancient benches and canny little shelves where bottles from Laurie Lee's beer collection would sit. There had always been a tatty and immovable little display promoting Laurie's books in the pub; now there were a number of subtle points scattered about the place ingraining his memory into the newly worn weave of its wood. The cellar was closed off and transformed into a kitchen. The old kitchen was opened into a bar area. Everything was smartened up and faded. It became the sort of pub one might imagine walking into if one were thirsty after a backward jaunt in a time machine.

All that the new-look old-style Woolpack lacked was a daily coat of sawdust on the floor and barrels on the bar, but there was no use for that sort of décor in a pub determined to sell food. The locals and drinkers were collected in the bar area as they always had been, grunting with pleasure as they stood in front of the open fire and steamed, but the rest of the pub was opened up for reservations, for attracting diners into the welcoming bosom of Slad.

All of a sudden, it went from a small village pub that served community and summertime tourists to a roaring success, constantly busy and attracting carloads of people. Dan's arty London crowd came roaring into the village and the posh set, the younger generations of the sort that Laurie had courted and counted as friends when in London, came tumbling down by train after them. People like Damien Hirst, Joe Strummer and Alex James were in and out of the pub and attracted a curious crowd who tagged along in their wake, hoping to be surprised.

Hirst was the most noticeable there, revelling in the much reported and now abandoned alcohol-fuelled phase of his public life. Not a gentlemanly man in his cups, he was known to preside over nights of anarchy in the pub, seeing whom he could persuade to play his drunken games or cow into dancing attendance. He was a decadent sprite in these moods, an argument on legs bundling through the pub demanding that people pay him attention, funny and caustic and disruptive.

I encountered him twice in the pub; the first time, I was introduced to him and he was not in the mood to be introduced. He barely acknowledged my presence. The second time was more combative. I had been in the pub for a while, watching the evening get ever more out of hand, drinking and concocting plans with friends. I got up to go to the bar, when a bespectacled figure appeared at my side.

'You're going to the bar!' said the figure, breathing alcohol fumes in my face. 'Get me a drink!'

I turned around. It was Hirst, looking at me intently.

'Get your own,' I said.

'I want a drink, you –'

'Well you know where the bar is!' I snapped, heat rising in my face. I walked off.

'I want a f***ing drink,' he yelled. I looked back. He was stopping someone else, and there seemed to be something of a performer's gait in the way he shuffled up to him, angry and amused at once. I didn't stop to see if he got his way. I left the pub, impatient, when the beer garden turned into a skittering host of people with mobile phone antennae sticking from their ears all apparently working for Hirst.

Celebrities, ill-behaved or otherwise, brought hangers-on, and wealthy types from London. That combination brought journalists, eager to discover what was going on in a quiet little valley, and they brought hastily assembled comparisons that ignored the valley's history. Slad was 'Notting Hill in Wellies' they decided, trumpeting it in the gossip and lifestyle section of the newspapers, with smiling photos of beautiful people gadding in the countryside. If *Cider with Rosie* was mentioned, it was in passing. The locals rebelled, started a counter-revolution, complaining that the village was becoming too busy and noisy, too fashionable, fearing that the publicity would lead to the sort of shift in population that Notting Hill itself had seen when the wealthy moved in and priced the black community out. They fretted, fulminated and worried that the pub was not serving the community as it had been hoped it would. They won. The Woolpack settled back into tranquillity and Slad breathed deeply, safe in the knowledge that no interloping celebrity or fashion would steal the limelight from its favourite son.

19

Coming Home

[These verses] speak for a time and a feeling which of course has gone from me, but for which I still have close affection and kinship.

Laurie Lee, in a note introducing his *Selected Poems*.

I spent eighteen years living outside the valley, carrying the memory of it locked into the shell of my skull, informed by the haphazard spirit of it: the sound of water crazing its way under the Roman bridge; the incessant hunting of the owls at the edge of dusk, hooting at the window like angry ghosts; the hush of rain in yew branches. I yearned for the qualified silence of it all, for the freedom from car-blare and late night homebound pub-stumbler shouting at lampposts. I longed for the noises I might add to that hiss of life: the delicate roar of steam from the kettle; the creak of metal as the fire takes hold in the wood-burning stove; the croak of a boot in mud, crossing the cattle-bound stream on the way to the Woolpack.

The house had became a portal for papers and whispers, mice and the creeping damp of silence; the sort of place that walkers considered lost, that required only shutters and a caved-in roof to become as derelict as Rosie Bannen's cottage. I often heard them, on my occasional visits, discussing our cottage in loud voices from the path, braying what a shame that it was 'abandoned and probably haunted'. I took perverse pleasure in coming face-to-face with them in the window as they peered in, pouncing up from my chair with a brusque 'Hallo' and watching as they reeled away startled, back to the path and the walk, hoping their hearts were pounding. A practical joke born of guilt.

How, then, to negotiate a return? Both my father and I had felt the call of the early years there ripping at our mouths like steel hooks, reeling us in, pulling us up too often into the sharp, hard-to-breathe air of maudlin nostalgia. It was difficult to go back – the paperwork drowning-pool was full of little currents and eddies that slowed its clearing, and my mother's presence felt constrained by our inability to clear it. All but a few of our human ties to Slad had gone. What remained was art, literature and the landscape itself. It sprawled out before me like a tangled map of loss.

A house is only as alive as the people who live in it, and we populated ours with paper and a rising aura of damp. We wrote about it, abstracted it, pushed the valley from its intrinsic reality and into an unsustainable utopian space. The more we quested after it, the farther away it seemed. It became a literary conceit, a bone of contention sticking out of the landscape at an awkward angle, rarely dealt with on a daily basis but never forgotten.

Then, one winter morning, I received a telephone call from Mrs Hopf, still living next door.

'There's someone in your house, Adam. He says he knows you. He's threatening to squat,' she said.

I ran to the pub to raise a posse, and found three friends ready to go and see off squatters – Legzee, Rhidian and Celine. We bundled into Rhidian's car, pumped up and ready for a confrontation. I held the front door keys rattling in my hand as we bombed out to the cottage in the early evening. Even before we got there, I felt a rising swell of elation – at last the cottage needed protecting. We were a ragtag bunch of defenders, but it seemed appropriate that Legzee was there, perhaps more than a little tipsy, having taken a few drinks after work, but all the same geared up to help. Arriving at the green tin garage, we spilled like fish from the net of the car, puffed down the path to the garden, checking and inspecting everything as we went, talking the language of disconcerted bravado. The adrenaline in my veins ran sharp. We got to the house and banged on the door: 'Are you in there, Al?' I called.

But the squatter had gone. He had taken his chances on a well-known empty house, but had not counted on the eagle eyes of neighbours who had come and quizzed him through the door and taken his number. He had begun to dismantle the lock and left it by the door, but after my father's follow-up call had offered to introduce the police into the equation, he had apparently fled. The only thing 'Al' left me other than a door to mend was the leverage I needed to move back in.

The cottage had survived eighteen years without a break-in (apart from Everest, climbing in through the kitchen window for a glass of water after a long walk on a hot day at almost the exact time two other friends were arriving to stay at the cottage for the weekend) and now I had all the impetus I needed to go back, to work on sorting it out and reclaiming it as a functional home.

Not so idyllic, living in a damp, cold house that's been standing empty but for mice and papers for eighteen years. I moved the bulk of my books and belongings back in the summer, and began the dusty and initially euphoric process of sifting through papers and making space to live, but did not move back in until the winter of 2012–13, bringing cats with me. As soon as I moved back in, the house and the valley began to take their revenge for long years of abandonment.

Winter set in with a vengeance, the worst I had endured since childhood, and I discovered that the chimney was blocked and the wood-burning stove had been rendered inoperable by time and alterations. It had been connected to the water supply when I was a child, but this had been disconnected three years before. So I all but froze through the long winter that lasted until April, unable to sit still long enough to write or think, bleeding money out of radiators and huddled into a sleeping bag with cats and hot water bottles pressed hard against my chest.

In 1985, when the snow had fallen so thick that the electricity failed, it had taken my father and me three hours to climb the hill out of the valley and seek refuge with the farmer. Cold and disheartened, we slogged up the path that runs past Driftcombe, falling into deep, treacherous drifts, slithering and unnerved. This time, I had no escape routes. The world pressed cold at the windowpanes and snow-cold night patterned the inner eyelids of the house with frost. I stayed for the cats, determined to reclaim the landscape or let it reclaim me.

The cats, a friend's beloved pair of tortoiseshell sisters, which she could no longer keep, were constantly harassed by next door's aggressively territorial black tomcat, who woke me night after night wailing and growling in the attic. He sprayed for dominance and terrorised the two nervous intruders I had brought to his turf until they fled – Frieda to who knows where, Freya to the chicken farm at the top of the hill, where she made herself at home beneath the roosts and drove the owners to distraction.

Poorly spayed, Freya took to marching from door to door around the cat-owning houses at the edge of Bisley parading herself for toms. Unable to reproduce but undergoing the fiercest of urges, she rubbed against garage doors, invaded houses, terrorised chickens, startled horses and upset the neighbourhood entirely with her frustrated sexuality. I caught her and repatriated her twice, tempting her with food from beneath the hay at the chicken farm the first time, only to be bitten savagely for my trouble. The second time, a man whose cat's food she'd been stealing cornered her in his house and locked the cat flap before calling me to come and carry her away. Freya treated the kitchen like an assault course until finally I cornered and calmed her, wearing toughened gardening gloves and a grimace. Two times I took her back and each time she ran straight off again, intimidated by the neighbour's cat, the damp, the cold.

Alone in the house, I left the cat flap open for weeks, putting down food in the hope that they'd return. The only visitor I had was next-door's cat, sour faced and frightened, eating greedily from the peace offerings I'd left. Come May, the cat flap was blocked, though every time I hear a cat's yowl in the garden now I rush to the window, hoping that either Frieda or Freya has returned.

In the snow, I rediscovered community via the generosity of neighbours who'd pick me up if they passed me slouching up the hill on foot, unable to cycle through the ice, who would listen and forgive if I pounded on their doors after a long walk home through blinding snow, suddenly uncertain if there were any people left alive in a world so consumed by soft bee-sized fists of falling ice.

It had not always been so welcoming. One set of neighbours, who bought the Old Chapel as a fixer upper, I only ever spoke with once on the phone after I discovered that their plans for extending the house reached ten feet into our garden. The officious husband called me out of the blue, aggressively justifying his plans after I'd spent an afternoon marching incredulous up and down the garden as Mrs Hopf explained them to me. These hellish neighbours were also prone, I discovered later, to come out and yell the riot act at walkers taking the public footpath past their house, Several members of the Lloyd family were caught in the blast of their ire and responded in kind, insisting furiously and derisively that they had been walking here all of their lives.

Combative and colonial to the last, the new owners had also bought some of the field below the house, which included the spring that had served the community until plumbing was installed in the 1950s. They denied all comers access to the spring and were attempting to have the land reassigned from agricultural to domestic use but, mercifully, left after a flurry of complaints to the planning department, which were so voluminous and came from so many quarters of Slad and Bisley that the people who moved to the house in their wake were apprehensive in case the valley turned out to be filled with a den of Gorgons who would go out of their way to make their lives miserable. The Mohammeds, however, were kind, and open, and were welcomed with open arms (though their black tomcat is still no friend of mine).

The valley under snow was less than welcoming. I explored where I could, sliding down paths that had been worn into perilous ruts by trail bikes, investigating walls that had in places all but vanished, their stones taken away and repurposed or simply cast down onto the path like Jericho's walls under the relentless biting music of the frost. The walkers' path to Slad down past the Roman bridge was blocked by an uncut tree that required a loose limbo dance to navigate past.

The field surrounding the Roman bridge was churned to mud and regularly blocked by a couple of cows who stood and stared at me with steely bewilderment, refusing to move. I read them poetry, or, if I was feeling cruel, sang. Sometimes it drove them off. Certainly it worked better than reason, to which frustration occasionally led me, keen to get to the pub and explaining this in irate detail to gawping bovines. Mostly, of course, loud noises worked, or climbing the stile in the hope that the cows would move. Even if the cows could be negotiated, the sucking soup of mud and effluent to which they churned the ground could take your boot off in an instant, as if your foot were merely a shucked pea. It made the first pint at the Woolpack feel like even more of a reward.

20

The Spring is Sprung

Bold with the longing of Spring went he
Into the danger he could not see.

From 'Spring Fox' by Frank Mansell

The sun always returns. Snows melt and relentless mud thickens into springy turf. Bitter pills of hail soften into warm rain, which hangs like spun glass in a glaze of light on tree branch and mossy stone, spider's web and eyelash. Winter is a state of mind as much as a season. Tree branches stretch their furled spears to the sun, which wait to become leaf, just as people reach out into the landscapes that surround them, struggle to be a part of them, and of each other, with the tender encouragement of spring.

Catkins hang like lambs' tails from birch and hornbeam; fat-headed snowdrops mooch in mutinous clusters, defying frost; daffodils poke their green stems skyward. Eventually coltsfoot and primrose cluster at the path's edge and an explosion of yellow welcomes in the longer days.

The thrush's tinder throat strikes up,
The sparrow chips hot sparks
From flinty tongue, and all the sky
Showers with electric larks.[1]

Night becomes a reward, a slow simmering promise of tomorrow's sunlight kissed against the tree line in streaks of red and orange every evening. The stream sings a slower song as rains recede and children laugh as they run into the gardens, their high voices clattering through the treetops as the birds puff themselves up and begin their mating rituals.

I wake often to deer in the garden, settled in like hounds under the boughs of trees where the rain won't reach them as they sleep, or peering through my door, inquisitive and easily startled. They bolt into the fields if I move too fast. In the absence of my cats, the trees are alive with tits and finches, small bolts of gold and blue shimmering through the evergreen yew after dizzy clouds of insects. The house is alive with insect life. A wasps' nest in the roof pours its skirmish-ready troops outwards if the sun is hot, or buzzing confused and lazy inwards if all the sun can do is heat the panes of glass. Opening windows, I startle hosts of ladybirds out of slumber; watch as they fleck the landscape red and black before vanishing into the vastness of the day.

Exploring the fields below the house comes as a shock. I remember picking my way through sheep and cattle, the occasional horse. Now they sit un-grazed, too remote to be worth fencing, the walls built during cloth trade plenty falling away like broken teeth. Old Captain George who farmed them has retired and they have become ragged, as if a giant tramp has lain down under his coat on them and passed into permanent sleep. They are treacherous; all that is left of the close-cropped turf I ran down as a child is a sheer path worn flat by walkers; the rest is tussock and sapling. The old ford that led to the badger's sett has grown over and been replaced with a polite and slippery wooden bridge, all stones removed. It feels too safe to walk this plank; I miss the shift of the stones beneath my feet; the

---

1 From 'Edge of Day' by Laurie Lee.

feeling of risk; the push of the water taking away any sensation of control. In wellingtons, I wade across instead, up to the edge of the wood to look across at the decorous acres of the racing stables where Captain George's son breeds winners and keeps the land tamed to prevent the horses turning their delicate ankles, frustrated that his land beyond the line of sight of tourists has become so ragged and unkempt that it risks turning to woodland and cutting off all line of sight to Slad.

Out of the woodwork the people came; I saw them as I passed the pub, walking into Stroud on the long route that allows for beer stops and conversation. Old faces, familiar and welcoming, clutching roll-ups and beer on the bench next to the road, hailing me as I walked past. New faces too, occupying old houses; my old friend Joe's sister-in-law Hester now lives in the house in which Laurie Lee grew up. She and her partner have been clearing, and planting snowdrops on, the steep bank down from the road that Annie Lee struggled up, perpetually late, to get the bus to town. They have been taming the garden with dry-stone walls and vegetables, keeping the essence of the house intact whilst keeping it habitable and free of floods.

Visiting, I could almost smell the food that Annie cooked on the stove a century before; the large fireplace was still nearly as it would have been then, stove blazing; the cellar was stacked with sustenance and felt cool as an autumn breeze. The attic bedroom that Laurie and his siblings had occupied felt changeless but for the modern furniture, occupied by children who bounced down the stairs to smile questioningly at me and vie noisily for their parents' attention as we chattered over mugs of tea.

I found myself, that spring, at a medieval feast in the farmstead on Knapp Lane below Swift's Hill, a feast followed by a showing of Pasolini's vulgar and ridiculous *Canterbury Tales*. I had walked through the woods to get there, high on wild garlic and the shuttering late May light rushing through the trees, down through Elcombe, laid out like random jawbones on an ossuary hill, and passing below Swift's Hill as birds flicked over it in insect frenzy, down into a gathering of people sitting at trestle tables, a hog roast by the barn. The farmyard was grassed over, and the barns were filled with chairs.

Laurie would have felt quite at home there, I suspected: the wine was being served by exquisite young women sporting diaphanous smiles, a preternatural gaiety shivering in their eyes; MPs rubbed shoulders with artists, farmers and country socialites; a duo played ancient, hypnotic folk music on droning, eccentric instruments, which cut through the chatter at exquisitely inappropriate moments; a jester gambolled through the crowd, dressed in black, performing aggravating slapstick and asking gnomic questions. Faces quickly began to glaze over with horror whenever he approached. Laurie would have put on his public face and held court, waving his white fedora in benediction and welcoming one and all to his valley, even the jester.

I was not so easy in the hot sun. I ate and drank, watched the film all the way through and turned at the end to find that I was almost the last person left, the only one not sober enough to care that Pasolini had traduced one of the great works of early English literature. I staggered from the barn the film had been show in, a high-raftered and draughty shell of Cotswold stone filled with theatre seats, and looked around. The beautiful serving girls were writing fire words on the night sky with sticks they lit in a brazier. I joined them, quietly drunken admiration fused with the need to play, to write, to create the valley anew out of darkness and fire. Eventually, I stumbled home through the woods, weaving through the night like one of those blazing sticks. I felt immortal, a perfect part of the valley, as alive as it was possible to feel when stumbling across motorbike tyre ruts, falling elated into pockets of wild garlic and finally crashing down the steep path from Keensgrove wood to the stream and home.

I woke in the front room the next morning giddy with hangover, birdsong hammering in my head. My clothes were stained green and black and stank of mud and night and garlic. I sat in the garden with a pen, under a tent of yew, and began to write.

As spring uncoiled into summer, I bought an electric bicycle, a new concession to modernity and the need to escape the confines of the valley to find work and food. A job came next, at the shop behind the garage that had delicately rejected me twenty years before, and the contract for a book.

I celebrated by cycling far and fast, sweeping through the lanes like Icarus, hell-bent on sunshine and freedom. Then, after the second day of work at the shop, cycling home late, driven faster by hunger, assuming, like Annie Lee, that there would be something or someone to catch me should I be unable to stop, I turned a corner and met an unexpected car. I hit the brakes and only the tarmac was there to catch me.

21

Tramadol with Rosie

A summer lost to two broken arms and three broken ribs, unable to write or cook or even wash without a severe amount of pain (after a week I had to be hosed down by my ex-girlfriend as she would not stand for me rapidly becoming riper than a blue cheese left to melt in Tupperware under a scalding sun). I was ripped away from the valley, taken in by friends, barely able to send a short text message on my mobile phone let alone write. I simmered and sweated as the summer turned into perfect walking weather and watched my opportunity to bask in all that the Slad Valley had to offer vanish under a blanket of pain relief. Doped up on Tramadol, I could barely even read and found myself gummed to the teat of the television most days, my delicately generous array of hosts doing their best to offer me comfort as I struggled to settle or find sleep.

The accident allowed me time to think, though, especially as I mended; to think about the valley and how I had come to spend my life entwined in a vision of it that was real and unreal at the same time. I was forced to re-evaluate, to scrumple up my imprac- tical poet's eye and consider a practical life more carefully. It was not enough to live there high on paper and aesthetics, admiring the mob of crows belting after buzzards or the soft breathy song of the wood pigeon. I had let the landscape rule me. That had to change, become a process of reconciliation, co-habitation.

I realised also how integral Laurie Lee had been to my under-standing of the valley, his writing and his brief but vital instructions running like a stream through my fields of thought. My father told me over the phone that I had, as a very small child, been entered into a poetry competition run by Goldenlay eggs, judged by Laurie, who had been delighted when it turned out I had won. Each time I met him, he had nudged me or bribed me towards poetry. Patterns of seed scattering came clear through the haze of opiates, the pound-ing rush of suffocated pain. He had, in his quiet way, helped me keep a sense of place rooted in my chest.

Looking back, I saw that at every turn he had been standing at the head of the Slad Valley like an overseer, laughing in the hot sun and encouraging others on. He even took some of the profits of *Cider with Rosie* and invested them back into the landscape, buying woodland to walk in, which has only just been sold by his estate to the Gloucestershire Wildlife Trust. The Trust started a campaign amongst their members to raise the funds to buy the land and keep it in perpetuity as an area of natural diversity; the response was overwhelming because of Laurie and *Cider with Rosie*. It was heart-ening to hear that sections of the valley were going back to a form of common land, to be cared for and admired for generations to come.

Part-mended, I arrived back in the valley in September, with a clearer vision of what needed to be done to make the house viable but with-out the energy to do it. I threw myself into work, creaking up the hill to the shop three days a week, exhausted from slowly weaning myself off the painkillers and afraid to tackle the bicycle, which had survived the accident undamaged but for a buckled wheel. It had had a soft landing, flipping me over and landing heavy on my ribs two months before.

I pushed hard, but still relied on friendship and goodwill to sur-vive: Charly, a friend from work, cleaned the cottage chimney and loaned me a new stove whilst my wood burner went in for repair;

I found a good-humoured tree surgeon by the name of Chris in the pub, who was willing to come and take back the overhanging fringe of yew. I watched as he swung up into the trees, his gangling ground-gait slipping away as the rope took him upwards with the saw into the fluid routines of work. My ex-girlfriend and her new partner brought free-cycled kitchen units and fitted them whilst I made tea, cheerfully insulting me for allowing my naturally untidy streak to become so amplified by such a poor excuse as broken bones. It was healing to watch the house get patched up and mended. I began to feel the mending affect my own physical condition, especially as I could now sit and read in the front room at night without the sensation of damp slithering like an invasion of slugs through my bones.

Now I am reaching past childhood to a new understanding of the way life in a small valley works. I am getting used to seeing Neil Rees stalking the lanes with a rifle, keeping the squirrel population down, standing in roadside shadow-edge as I cycle home from work at dusk. Dogs bark in the distance and lights flicker on and off. Arriving at the house, the memory of my mother shivers like birdsong at the window. The stream crackles in the distance as I open the front door. 'Birdsong and water bear away grief.'[1]

My father comes back to the valley occasionally, bearing the city's fire like a brand before him, even at seventy-eight. Sheep appear briefly in the fields opposite the house, surprising escapees from who knows which field. Like storm-blown clouds they vanish again the next day, taking clumps of overgrown grass away in their bellies. The jay screams through the wood, still laughing, perhaps, at my childhood conviction that it was a hoopoe. A pair of buzzards patrols the rim of trees. Pat Hopf still lives in the cottage at the other end of the terrace from me, keeping the garden clear with the help of her sons and offering gin and history whenever I call by. Friends come and go, old and new faces, some of them in tiny, mewling form. The world seems small and huge at once.

I am pleased to find that the rusted bicycle I pulled from the rotting garden shed and left parked in hewn yew branches has been

---

[1] From 'Old Song' by Frances Horovitz.

secretly coveted by the teenager living up the hill in Katy's old house. He calls by occasionally, talks about music. The bike is his now, under repair and soon to be ridden to school once more, after twenty-five years of neglect. His name is Laurie. It seems appropriate to pass this long-neglected wheeled frame of freedom on to him.

SOLSTICE

The wood is cut and darkness sighs
its needle shower of yew-green light,
of brown stems in the ragged hedge.
Stars pucker on the cusp of sight
and, startling from the woodland's edge,
the moon is an owl; its cries

changing the track of the sea.
The stream sings out in reverse,
a song of solidness, of creak,
as if water needed to rehearse
the change of seasons, or to speak
a human tongue in sympathy.

I hum the water's song, the shallow
breath that shatters on the path
in footsteps, startling a deer,
then slide indoors to wood the hearth
and spark an answer to the fear
of winter; a flickering hallow

that scatters the long night's shadow up the wall
and frees me, briefly, from the vixen's numbing call.

22

Coda

When we are very young almost everything we say is poetry, of a kind. The words that form on our tongues are shaved down strips of meaning reduced to the bare essentials. We pick up and run with refrains learned from our surroundings, dadaists to the core, building intelligence out of the noises we do not fully understand, and our parents sing it back to us, delighted in our soundscapes of erupting understanding.

We imitate and accumulate, robbing the landscape of whatever is closest to us, be it bird song or tractor's growl, car horn or television, song or silence. We make music and meaning of our surroundings until we are able to sculpt ourselves a grammar and communicate fully, in solid functionality – and beyond if we dare push ourselves that far.

I count myself indelibly fortunate to have grown up in the outer reaches of Slad, to have been surrounded by birdsong, the aching screech of the vixen, the brutish rustle of the badgers I watched at play with my mother, secreted upwind in the early evening at the edge of Catswood, opposite Snows Farm.

When I was a child the valley was perpetually alive with songs and sounds, and it was alive with poetry, instilled in me by both of my parents and by the valley itself. It still is, to a great extent. I grew up wired for the sound of language and how it interacted with nature, in a long, lyrical song of landscape that was started by Laurie Lee and which has kept on being sung in rounds, in one form or another, around and about the valley ever since. More and more people are taking it up as the urban world attempts to swallow our understanding of what it means to be alive.

All landscapes have their music, but Slad is fortunate to have had a singer as tender and profoundly understanding of its moods and temperaments and lyrical weather patterns as Laurie Lee. The villagers and the valley have responded in kind, by keeping his song alive, either in the hands of poets and artists or in the more prosaic actions of people determined to preserve whatever is left of the lost innocence and experiences that Laurie mourned in *Cider with Rosie*. And it is not only the village; the people of Stroud on the whole recognise how much this glacier-carved lung of land means to the area, and how much it would damage us all if it were swallowed alive brick by brick, as do the people his work has touched all over the world.

The rapacious road that runs through the village cannot be changed, and nor should it be. It is too late to save all but a few of the farm jobs that withered away after the Second World War. Yet even the people who own 4x4 cars that glisten like seals fresh from the surf, who leave halogen lights on outside their houses long into the night to torture moths and who snarl at walkers who trundle past their gates have bought into the song of Slad that Laurie started, have come here for an idyll, albeit one they sometimes seem a little less than willing to share, an idyll that is at once divorced from the world and a part of it.

Poetry has made a playground of the valley, be it Laurie's, Frank Mansell's or my family's. It is no longer a place of dung and chickens in the yard, of dirty-faced boys running out of school to follow a coffin up into the church. Only the field above the racing stables still stinks of the past, where piles of dung-laden hay from the stable floors are dumped in the field at the entrance to Trillgate, steaming and reeking in the summer sun. The old boundaries are shifting and crumbling away. Old stone walls lie in ruin, like smashed jaws on the borders of the fields, consumed by a cancer of fences and badly maintained hedgerows. Trees jut from them at impossible angles. Roots thicker than legs ride them like horses. In the twenty-first century, the wealth of the valley is kept within doors more often than not.

It is impossible to keep cows or sheep in the farther-flung fields below the house I grew up in because no one will fence them, and they're too steep for racing horses, so hassocks of grass grow rampant in the fields I ran through as a child, an impediment to walkers. The Gloucestershire Wildlife Trust owns some of them, and those are easier to access for walkers and visitors, for all that they are a protected haven for wildlife. The landscape of Slad is being recast as a place of ease, a new world to escape to from the city, and this necessarily means that the difficulties of the countryside are being gently erased. Muddy fords over the streams are replaced with wooden planks, taking some of the risk and joyful terror out of walking. No more mud to the knee for the incautious walker who doesn't test the next stone they must step on.

Poetry and the impulses that drive all of creation are too often chased from us as we grow up, as the daily grind drags us farther and farther from our imaginative roots and imposes the grammar of necessity upon us. It is marvellous, then, to find places that still carry us back to the imitative shrilling of childhood, and a sense of ease, where people of all stripes still mingle and laugh and pull together regardless of their upbringing or relative wealth and, although the accents have shifted to the point that the local dialect is a welcome surprise rather than a common occurrence and many of the houses are occupied by bankers, artists or the retired, and although a certain sentimentalism about Slad hangs from the branches of memory, fat as a harvest moon, it remains just as important to remember the valley as it was, as it is to cherish it now: a place where gentle rural anarchy meets arch conservatism and thrives in the face of relentless urban progress.

Not for nothing did John Papworth and Leopold Kohr, two of the people who helped inspire E.F. Schumacher's *Small is Beautiful*, live in or visit this valley. According to Schumacher: 'Today, we suffer from an almost universal idolatory of giantism. It is therefore nec-

essary to insist on the virtues of smallness – where this applies.'
The virtues of smallness are most abundant in Slad. It is a community that relies on its smallness, even now when it is connected to
the rest of the world and has long been separated from Laurie Lee's
childhood. It is that childhood, the mythic smallness of it and its
lyrical retelling, that helps keep Slad and its thumb offshoots free of
wanton development.

Even today, when building firms try and press through proposals
for hundreds of houses on the outskirts of Stroud leading in to the
Slad Valley, they find themselves forced by Laurie's reputation into
offering concessions such as creating wild spaces at the bottom of
their developments. Protestors, invigorated by Laurie's wry spirit,
counter this by pointing down at the sprawling fields and saying:
'We've got all the wild spaces we need! Let them be.'

Laurie's vision was a quiet one, but it has remained persuasive to
the point that he has become part of the landscape, a point of refer-
ence for people all over the world, even for people who have not read
him. Schoolgirls and tourists will now find him buried in the valley
rather than in a pint at the Woolpack, but only his body is buried
between the church and the pub, and from there, only we look out
at the valley. What matters of Laurie is buried in the landscape and
in the people who live and work in the valley; a spark, a seed, a fragment of lyricism and light.

If Slad and the valleys that surround it can remain as a preserva-
tion point, where futurist meets deep ecologist and has a pint or
three in the Woolpack with labourer, artist and celebrity, all determined to protect the landscape and community for its own sake,
and for the sake of later generations, rather than because it matters
just to them, then we will all be Laurie Lee in a small way, thousands
of us, if only for a night, propping up the bar with a vision of Albion
that can be translated to all the remaining wild spaces that are left to
us, and that need to be maintained if we are to retain as a nation a
sense of what our past is and what our future may be.

ROOTS

For Kate Johnson

A last gauzed smile of winter
fades from the valley. Snowdrops
stoop like downtrodden ghosts
along the Hopf's immaculate garden path.
The few adventurous daffodils that shivered
into hopeful bud twelve days ago, then froze,
creak through the last of March
like green, thawing icicles, releasing
a long preserved insect's breath of sun.

I walk up the hill as I always did
towards your old house, lost
in the high, shrill calls of us as children,
when this valley was ours.
It dreamt us into being, I think; the rough-champed slope,
the stream, the pockets of woodland
that were our other homes, the brambling dens
which felt real as built stone in late spring sun.
        All that has changed

though not for better or for worse.
There are no judgement calls
in nature. Only what is, and what will be.
You with your four children
called to the sea, the youngest's white hair flying
as yours did when we ran the steep hill
down to the Roman bridge in outsized t-shirts,
hand in hand aged five and six.
I, alone now in the changed valley,